Made to Marvel

Made to Marvel

52 Family Devotions Exploring the Wild Wonders of God's Creation

ERYN LYNUM

Revell
a division of Baker Publishing Group
Grand Rapids, Michigan

Published by Revell
a division of Baker Publishing Group
Grand Rapids, Michigan
RevellBooks.com

Printed in the United States of America

Library of Congress Cataloging-in-Publication Data
Names: Lynum, Eryn author
Title: Made to marvel : 52 family devotions exploring the wild wonders of God's creation / Eryn Lynum.
Description: Grand Rapids, Michigan : Revell, a division of Baker Publishing Group, [2026] | Includes bibliographical references.
Identifiers: LCCN 2026004060 | ISBN 9780800748500 paperback | ISBN 9781493455584 ebook
Subjects: LCSH: Families—Prayers and devotions
Classification: LCC BV255 .L968 2026
LC record available at https://lccn.loc.gov/2026004060

Cover illustration by Sabrina Luoni
Cover design by Laura Klynstra

Baker Publishing Group publications use paper produced from sustainable forestry practices and postconsumer waste whenever possible.

26 27 28 29 30 31 32 7 6 5 4 3 2 1

For my dad, Alan Fiebig
April 12, 1960–December 5, 2025
To whom I'm forever grateful for pointing me
to the truth of God's Word
and the marvels of his creation

Contents

You Were Made to Marvel

Do you know what it means to *marvel*?

Marvel can be both a thing and an action.

A marvel is something that is wonderful. We might react to one, saying, "Wow! That sunset is a marvel."

When we marvel, we're overwhelmed by how wonderful something is. It might fill our heart with joy and curiosity at the same time. This happens a lot when we're out exploring God's wild and wonderful world. We might say, "I marvel at this beetle. It's so neat!"

God created you to marvel at his marvelous creation, to "stop and consider God's wonders" (Job 37:14 NIV).

This book is an adventure through God's creation. In it, we'll discover his detailed designs in creatures, plants, and other natural wonders you might have right around where you live. As we uncover creation's details, we'll also unearth important truths about God, our great Creator. We'll be learning from his two books—Scripture and creation—together.

Many mysteries of nature are tucked in these pages that, once solved, can make us laugh, smile, delight in, and worship God. You might be surprised by what you learn about "common" things. Even natural things that seem simple are not simple at all but have been masterfully engineered to work well and to cause us to marvel. As you venture through these pages, highlight or draw a star next to everything that amazes you or that you didn't expect.

Are you ready to marvel? Let's hit the trail!

How to Use This Book

A great way to use this book is to set it down often.

As you read about and discover God's handiwork in nature, may it inspire you to step outside, explore, and marvel at his creation right where you live—and then come back to these pages for more.

There are fifty-two chapters in this book, one for each week of the year. Each chapter includes an illustration, a deep dive into God's designs, and truth from God's Word. You can adventure through each chapter in order or skip ahead to learn about something you have recently seen or are curious about. If you'd like to explore chapters by topic, use the Explore by Topic guide in the back of the book to study mammals, birds, insects, reptiles, amphibians, fish, invertebrates (creatures without backbones), plants, earth science, and geology.

As you enjoy a chapter, take that week to learn more about and perhaps even find the creature, plant, or other thing in nature. The Time to Explore activity in each chapter offers inspiration for exploring God's wild and wonderful world. Throughout each devotion you will find some scientific words in italics that we might not use every day. You can find simple definitions of those words in the glossary at the end of the book.

Adventure at your own pace and in your own direction. There are no rules to this book so long as it draws you deeper into God's creation and causes you to marvel at all he's made.

You can explore further with my family's podcast for families: *Nat Theo: Nature Lessons Rooted in the Bible*. Find us at TheNaturalTheologyProject.com/nattheo. Listen on our website or on Apple Podcasts, Spotify, or Amazon Music, or watch on YouTube.

Organizing God's Creation

God designed more creatures than we will ever know about. Some have gone extinct, while others are still being discovered. Psalm 104:24 says,

> How many are your works, LORD!
> In wisdom you made them all;
> the earth is full of your creatures. (NIV)

We can see God's artistic style throughout nature. Some creatures share certain features, yet each one is unique. To help us understand the living things God has made, scientists have sorted them into groups. This human-made system of organization is called taxonomy.

Throughout this book, we'll mention some of these categories, so it will help to understand the seven main levels of taxonomy. The seven levels, in order, are kingdom, phylum, class, order, family, genus, species.

Each level becomes more specific as you go. Kingdom is a very broad category. For example, the animal kingdom includes all the animals God has made—flying, swimming, crawling, creeping, and more (including insects). As you move down through the levels, the groups become more specific. Species is the most specific category of taxonomy, and it tells us exactly what a creature or plant is.

Remember, God did not create these categories, and they do not limit his creativity. Some creatures surprise us and don't fit neatly into a category (like the platypus!). Taxonomy is simply a system people made to better understand the details of what God has created.

1

Salamander

Everything from Nothing

Raining Salamanders

Have you ever heard someone say that it's raining cats and dogs? This is a silly saying that means it is raining very hard outside. When people say this, they don't actually mean cats and dogs are falling from the sky. But long ago, people believed salamanders *did* rain down on the land. This, of course, sounds ridiculous to us. Still, it was their best explanation for how salamanders appeared, seemingly out of nowhere, after it rained. We now understand that salamanders appear after rain because they need moisture. They are more active after rainfall than in dry times, because they can easily dry out if they spend too much time in the sunshine without access to water.

Salamanders might look like lizards, but they are not. Lizards are reptiles with dry scales. Salamanders, on the other hand, are a type of amphibian with smooth, wet skin. They are more like frogs and toads (which are also amphibians) than lizards. Many types of salamanders breathe through their skin, a process known as ***cutaneous respiration***, which is how they get the oxygen they need to survive. If their skin is too dry, they cannot breathe well.

Vernal Pond Life

Salamanders sometimes come out after rainfall to find a place to lay their eggs. Salamanders lay eggs in ***vernal ponds***. A vernal pond is a temporary pond that contains water for only part of the year. Because vernal ponds are sometimes dry, fish do not live there, which gives a salamander's eggs a better chance of surviving. But what happens to the eggs that survive?

Salamander eggs hatch into babies called ***larvae***. Like toad and frog babies (called tadpoles), salamander babies spend their first stage of life in the water. They have fins and gills to help with swimming and breathing. As they grow older, they go through a big change called ***metamorphosis***, when they grow into their adult form. As adults, most species can come up on land, although a few species spend their whole lives in streams, rivers, lakes, and ponds.

Appearing Act

Once scientists discovered how salamanders lay eggs in vernal ponds and why they emerge after rainfall, the mystery of this curious amphibian was solved. The idea of salamanders raining from the sky sounds silly now. However, there have been many ideas like this throughout history.

Before scientists had the technology and knowledge to understand where some creatures came from, they thought they came out of nowhere. This idea is called ***spontaneous generation***, and it is the opposite of a disappearing act—it's an appearing act!

Another example of the spontaneous generation theory is with flies. Scientists noticed flies and baby flies (maggots) on rotting food or garbage. They believed the maggots and flies must have come from the waste itself, appearing like magic. Fly eggs were too small to see without a microscope, and they did not understand that flies often lay eggs on rotting meat or other garbage, which then hatch into maggots that grow into adult flies.

As science has advanced and new technologies have been developed, we've discovered so much more about the wonderful ways God designed living things.

Time to Explore

Go on a nature walk and look for a vernal pond, or ask an adult for help researching if there are some near where you live. Vernal ponds can be in the forest, where water pools after rainfall. They can also be found in rock depressions, like a pocket in a boulder. If it's spring or summer, a vernal pond might have amphibian eggs or other creatures inside, like freshwater shrimp. See how many creatures you can find. Can you identify any of them?

Everything from Nothing

Salamanders come from eggs that are laid underwater. But at one time, salamanders really did come from nothing besides God's word. God created all the creatures from the power of his word. The Latin phrase ***ex nihilo*** (pronounced *ex NEE-huh-low*) is often used in theology, which is the study of God and the Bible. *Ex nihilo* means that something was made from nothing.

When God created all the creatures, he designed everything through the creative power of his word rather than by using existing materials.

When we create a painting, we first gather materials such as paintbrushes, paints, a canvas or piece of paper, and water. When we make a cake, we need ingredients like flour, sugar, eggs, and oil. But God created everything from nothing, using no existing materials or ingredients. As he spoke all of nature into reality, he invented all the colors, textures, shapes, and the math needed for all the creature designs. Hebrews 11:3 says, "It is by faith we understand that the whole world was made by God's command so what we see was made by something that cannot be seen."

Think about how God created salamanders. As he did, he made them able to reproduce by laying eggs in vernal ponds to hatch into new salamanders. It took humans thousands of years to discover where salamanders come from, but God has known all along, for he designed this amazing process at the beginning of creation. Science and the study of nature take a while to catch up with God's designs, but what a fun and rewarding experience it is to discover things God made long ago!

Dear God, thank you for designing so much life in temporary vernal ponds, including salamanders. We love discovering your creativity in nature. Your word is so powerful, and by it you spoke all the creatures into being so we can marvel at the wonders you've made. Amen.

2

Skunk

The Least of These

What's That Smell?

Have you ever been riding in a car or on a bike and smelled something . . . not pleasant? Maybe you thought right away, *That's a skunk!* Skunks are well-known for their smelliness. But despite their reputation, they are magnificent creatures that God designed for meaningful work. Before we look at a skunk's job, let's explore how and why they smell.

Skunks do not always smell bad. They only spray foul smells when they feel threatened. The smelly substance comes from two ***glands***, like pockets, near the base of their tail. When they sense danger, they will lift their tail, point their rear end toward their predator, and spray—but not before giving a warning. Skunks typically resort to using their spray only if their warning signs of stomping their feet, lifting their tail, and hissing are not heeded.

Skunks are part of a large group of mammals called ***Musteloidea***, which also includes weasels, mink, and otters. Many animals in this group have scent glands that they use to communicate. Some also use scent for defense, like the skunk.

Keeping Tidy

Even though skunks are often thought of as smelly, they are exceptionally clean animals. They regularly groom themselves and can be litter-trained like a cat. In the wild, skunks prefer to use one area as their restroom. They also keep a tidy home underground, called a burrow. Appreciating their cleanliness can help us adopt a new attitude toward these fantastic creatures.

A Fine Tuxedo

It's not wise to observe a skunk closely in the wild, but have you ever seen a picture or video of one? Skunks are handsome animals. With their sleek black-and-white coats of fur, they look as though they are dressed up in a tuxedo, always ready for a fancy event. Their tails are a plume of beautiful, long, black and white hairs. We should work to see past a skunk's smelly reputation to the beautiful ways God has clothed it.

Keeping Nature in Balance

Skunks are not only tidy and handsome but they also keep God's creation in balance. God designed everything in nature to work together in perfect harmony. However, when sin's curse broke the world, nature became off-balance. One example of this is when insects devour too many crops that farmers work hard to grow as food for animals and humans.

Revelation 21:5 promises that God is making all things new. One day, his creation will be in perfect balance, and it will be more wonderful than we can imagine. But what about right now? God designed many creatures to help restore and protect balance, including skunks.

Skunks eat many insects that would otherwise destroy crops. They feast on grasshoppers, grubs, caterpillars, and beetles. Skunks are active and hunt at night, when insects are cold and become slower, making it easier for skunks to prey on them. Skunks are one of the most helpful mammals for keeping insect populations in balance. They also eat mice, further protecting farmers' crops and stored grains as well as keeping barns and homes mice-free. Skunks will snack on chicken eggs when they have the opportunity, but this is a small price to pay for all their helpful pest control.

Rather than seeing skunks as stinky creatures, many farmers welcome them, knowing the important role they play in balancing nature and protecting crops.

Time to Explore

Can you draw a skunk's fancy coat of hair? With permission from a trusted adult, find a photo of a skunk online or in a book. See if you can draw the skunk's body with its special striped tuxedo.

The Least of These

Have you ever seen someone treated wrongly? When Jesus was on earth, he often spent time with outcasts and people others looked down on. Jesus doesn't see like we often do. Instead, he sees the true value of every person because they are made in the image of God.

First Samuel 16:7 says, "God does not see the same way people see. People look at the outside of a person, but the Lord looks at the heart."

Consider how many people view skunks as stinky pests, while farmers see them as helpful coworkers. Similarly, Jesus gives us an example of caring for those who are looked down upon and suggests we look for their true God-given value. In Matthew 25:35–40, he says:

> I was hungry, and you gave me food. I was thirsty, and you gave me something to drink. I was alone and away from home, and you invited me into your house. I was without clothes, and you gave me something to wear. I was sick, and you cared for me. I was in prison, and you visited me.
>
> Then the good people will answer, "Lord, when did we see you hungry and give you food, or thirsty and give you something to drink? When did we see you alone and away from home and invite you into our house? When did we see you without clothes and give you something to wear? When did we see you sick or in prison and care for you?"
>
> Then the King will answer, "I tell you the truth, anything you did for even the least of my people here, you also did for me."

While we shouldn't invite a skunk into our home, we can look for ways to care for people who are in need or who are looked down on. As we do so, we are serving God. Consider ways you can bless someone today through a smile, a kind word, or a helping hand.

Dear God, thank you for creating skunks in amazing ways that help keep nature in balance. You created us for good works also. Help us to serve those in need. Amen.

3

Bat

Turn Your Ear

One of a Kind

Bats are often misunderstood. Many people find bats frightening and strange, but they are wonderfully created and have an important role in God's creation. God created bats to be gardeners. Some bats visit flowers to drink sweet nectar, and as they do, they spread pollen so more plants can grow. Other bats eat fruit and, later, they deposit it somewhere else, leaving behind seeds that can grow into new plants.

Even though bats fly, they are not birds. Bats are a type of ***mammal***. Mammals are animals that have hair or fur, are warm-blooded, and have a backbone. Most give birth to their live young and nurse their babies with milk. God created bats one of a kind because they are the only mammal that can fly.

Expert Aviators

One of my family's favorite summertime activities is sitting on our back deck after dusk and watching bats fly through our backyard. In some ways, bats fly better than birds. Unlike a bird's wing, which mostly stays the same shape, a bat's wing is its hand, which also means it is more flexible. Just as you can bend your fingers and close your hand, a bat can change the shape of its wing to bend and twist, helping the bat make tight turns when flying. God engineered bats as expert aviators that can twist, dive, and even somersault in the air to catch insects while flying. Some types of bats catch insects in their wings while flying like you might capture insects in a net. Some will also use the thin skin membrane between their hind legs and tail (called an ***uropatagium*** or ***interfemoral membrane***) as an insect net while flying.

Listen with Care

Has anyone ever said you are a good listener? Bats are excellent listeners because their lives depend on their ability to hear. Bats have to navigate dark skies and find insects to eat, and they do this primarily by using sound.

God designed bats to use ***echolocation***, a process of sending out chirping sounds that are so high in pitch that we humans cannot hear them. (If we could, we might go deaf!) The sounds help the bat locate prey by bouncing off its target, such as an insect. The echo returns to the bat's ear and brings with it a lot of helpful information.

God dialed in a bat's echolocation so well that echoes can help a bat know the

- size of its prey;
- shape of its prey; and
- direction in which its prey is moving.

To help his creations echolocate well, God designed bats with incredible listening skills. A bat's ear is designed with a special piece called a ***tragus***. Humans also have a tragus. It is the small bump in front of the opening of your ear. While our tragus helps our ears collect sound, a bat's tragus is designed specifically for echolocation so it can use its sense of hearing to "see" the world around it.

The tragus is not the only way God designed bats to listen carefully. The shape of a bat's ear is molded just right to collect sounds. Some species can even reshape their ears to hear best in different conditions. Bats also turn their ears in rapid and precise movements to locate exactly where sounds are coming from.

With perfectly shaped ears and the ability to reshape and turn them, bats listen with care and thrive in God's design.

Time to Explore

Go outside after dusk and see if you can spot bats twisting and diving through the air. How many can you see? Bats are most active in warm months when there are plenty of insects to eat. They sleep during the day and are active at night. The best time to watch them is after the sun has gone down, when the sky is quite dark but still light enough to spot their dark shapes flying rapidly against the sky. You might also spot them over a pond, lake, or pool as they swoop down to skim the water's surface for a drink while flying.

Turn Your Ear

Bats must turn their ears carefully to echolocate well and find what they need. God wants us to listen closely to find what we need too: not insects but wisdom.

Proverbs is a book in the Bible that is full of wise sayings and teachings. Proverbs 2:2 encourages us to turn our ears toward wisdom. Can you think of ways to do that? Here are some ideas:

- Surround yourself with wise people who follow God and know his Word.
- Avoid books, movies, or music that talk about foolish things or things that go against God.
- Listen to Bible lessons at church so you become more familiar with God's truth.
- Hide God's Word in your heart by memorizing Scripture.

Deuteronomy 30:20 says to listen to God's voice and hold fast to him. Do you think bats become better insect hunters with more practice? It makes sense that they improve as they listen for insects and find them in the night sky. In the same way, we can practice listening for truth and wisdom. God's Holy Spirit helps us with this. As you turn your ear toward wisdom, you will recognize it quicker, like a bat fine-tuning its listening skills.

If you see bats hunting insects, picture their ears rapidly turning to gather the information they need. Remember that God wants you to turn your ear toward wisdom and his truth so you can find what you need in life.

Dear God, thank you for making bats to help spread pollen and seeds. Help us to turn our ears to your wisdom each day. Train our ears to listen to your words in the Bible. Amen.

4

Daisy

It's in the Details

How Many Flowers?

If I were to hold up a daisy like the one in the illustration and ask, "How many flowers am I holding?" how would you answer?

It is a bit of a trick question, as what appears to be one flower is actually dozens to hundreds of flowers on a single stem. Daisies, along with sunflowers and chrysanthemums, are called ***composite flowers***. Composite means something is made of many parts, and that is true of daisies and flowers like them. They are not simple but instead have many tiny parts that reflect the intelligence and creativity of their excellent designer. How exactly is a single daisy many flowers?

If you look closely at the head of a daisy, or the colorful part on top of the stem, you will notice a center disk surrounded by what looks like delicate flower petals, but those are not petals; they are individual flowers called ***ray flowers***. They might look just like silky oval petals, but each "petal" is an individual flower. Inside the ray flower frame, in the center disk, there are ***disk flowers***.

A Daisy's Frame

Why is a daisy made up of both ray and disk flowers? Besides adding a beautiful frame around the flower, ray flowers are believed to attract pollinating species. They act like a large sign or banner (and are sometimes called ***banner flowers***), almost as if to call out to insects, "Hey! Over here! Come gather some sweet nectar!" Of course, a flower cannot talk or even think, but God designed composite flowers with large, showy ray flowers to help insects find them more easily. The ray flowers also act as a landing spot for insects to plop down on so they can get at the nectar inside the center disk flowers. Do you know why a flower needs insects to visit it?

Why Flowers Need Insects

God designed flowers to make more flowers with the help of insects. Inside a flower is sweet nectar liquid, which is an important food source for insects. When insects visit flowers to get the nectar, a flower's powdery pollen rubs off and sticks to the insect. The insect then flies away to visit another flower.

If it lands on the same type of flower as the first, and the pollen falls or rubs off, that flower can then make a seed.

Some flowers, including daisies, can pollinate themselves without the help of insects in a process called ***self-pollination***. However, it's more helpful when insects spread pollen from flower to flower in a process called ***cross-pollination***, which brings more genetic diversity and health to future flowers.

At the Center of It All

Do you remember the two types of flowers in a composite flower? We learned about the beautiful ray flowers, which look like petals. Inside the ray flowers, at the center of the daisy's head, are tiny disk flowers. Disk flowers hold the daisy's nectar. While the petallike ray flowers of most species cannot produce seeds, the center disk flowers can. I love watching composite flowers like the daisy throughout the summer as their disk flowers change shape. Early in the season, they are tiny, tight buds arranged like a spiral (called a ***Fibonacci spiral***, which is one of God's artistic styles of a spiral seen throughout nature). Throughout the summer, the disk flowers begin to blossom. The ones near the outer edge (close to the ray flowers) open first, moving inward toward the center, further highlighting the beautiful spiral pattern at the daisy's center.

When the disk flowers open, the nectar inside becomes accessible, and insects begin stopping by for a sweet drink.

Time to Explore

Find a daisy and look closely at its center disk flowers and outer ray flowers. A small magnifying lens or jewelry loupe can help you study the fine details. Can you count the ray flowers around the outer edge? Are the disk flowers in the center tightly closed in buds, or have they blossomed, welcoming pollinating insects to come collect nectar and spread pollen?

It's in the Details

God's Word is one big book made of many detailed parts, like a daisy. Did you know that every story in Scripture is connected? Just as we might place a magnifying lens over a daisy to see its tiny disk flowers, we can look closely at Scripture and see God's details.

His Word never changes, but we can discover truths in it that we have never seen before. I have been learning about the Bible for around thirty years, including going to college to study the Bible. Yet I discover new details all the time.

If we walk quickly by a daisy, we'll miss its details, and the same is true about God's Word. What are some ways you can practice looking at the details of God's Word? Here are some ideas:

- Read the same passage a few days in a row and ask God through prayer to show you new details you didn't see before.
- Highlight words or ideas in Scripture that stand out to you.
- Memorize or sing Scripture.
- Use a Bible concordance to study specific words in Scripture.
- Use a tool like a Strong's Bible Dictionary or BlueLetterBible.com to look at the original Greek and Hebrew definitions in a verse.
- Spend time in God's Word every day.

There is a study called ***hermeneutics*** that is all about diving deep into the Bible and interpreting what it means. I took a hermeneutics class in college, but it's never too early to begin looking closely at the Bible's details. When I was a child, I sat in sermons at church with a binder, notebook pages, and pens so I could take careful notes.

We can practice hiding God's Word in our hearts, as Psalm 119:11 encourages, and we can practice being those who understand and use God's Word rightly, as we read in 2 Timothy 2:15: "Do your best to present yourself to God as one approved, a worker who does not need to be ashamed and who correctly handles the word of truth" (NIV).

Dear God, thank you for fashioning flowers just right with all their many details. We are so grateful you give us comfort and instructions for life in your Word, the Bible. Help us to love your Word and study its details each day. Amen.

5
Dragonfly

Possible by Design

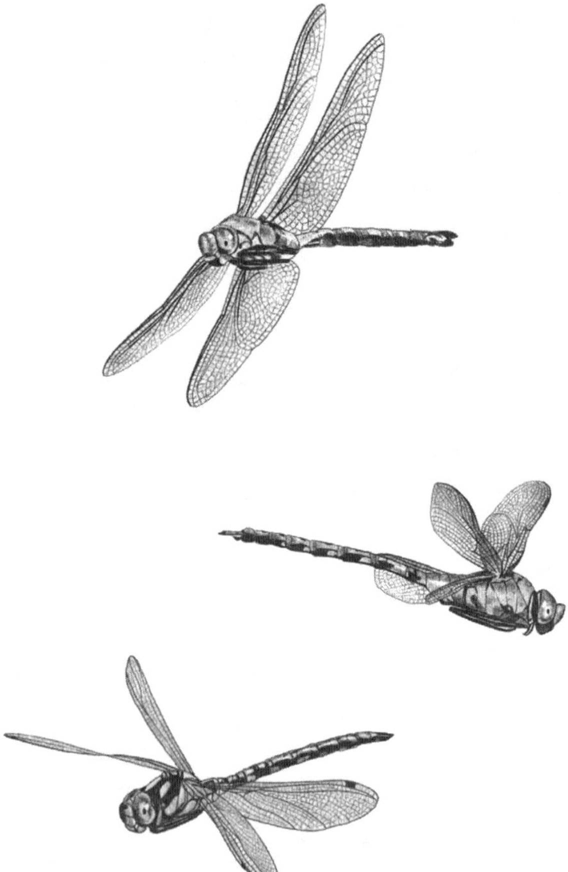

Designed to Fly

Have you ever watched a dragonfly zipping through the air, turning sharply, or hovering in place? They can even fly backward! By simply watching a dragonfly, you know it can fly. But how? Observations like these lead us to marvel at God's designs.

Bird flight is magnificent and has taken scientists a long time to study and understand. Insects, including the dragonfly, fly very differently from birds. Insect flight is a unique and exciting study.

Does a dragonfly have the same number of wings as a bird? Dragonflies have two sets of two wings, equaling four wings total. This is a very different design from birds, so we can expect that the dragonfly has distinct and special ways of flying.

A dragonfly's front wings are called ***forewings***, and its back wings are called ***hindwings***. Each of its four wings can move on their own (instead of always moving together). Each wing is attached to its own ***direct flight muscle***. Using these special muscles, a dragonfly can change the angle, speed, and rotation of each wing, making the dragonfly an incredible stunt flyer.

Brainy Wings

Picture a dragonfly zipping through the air while hunting its next meal, which it captures while flying, or swiftly dodging a bird that wants to eat it. Or imagine a gust of wind threatening to push the dragonfly off course. It could be tough to know how to control each of its four wings while flying and reacting to everything around it. What direction should each wing face at every moment? If a bird swoops too close, how should it adjust the rotation or speed of each wing? Thankfully, the dragonfly can fly with master precision because God designed it with brainy wings. This doesn't mean each wing has a brain—like it has its own direct flight muscle; instead, each wing has many tiny sensors that send important messages to the dragonfly's brain.

These sensors provide real-time data. Among many things, the sensors can tell the dragonfly about any tiny air pressure change around the wings. As the brain receives these messages, it then controls each direct flight muscle to rapidly respond to the information. Using this design, dragonflies fly by feeling but not by emotions or well-wishes. They fly by sensing the changes around their wings and using that information to rapidly adjust their flight.

Creating Tiny Tornadoes

Have you ever flown a kite and watched it soar on the wind only to have it lose its lift and crash down to the ground? By watching a dragonfly's incredible stunts, we can wonder how it twists, turns, hovers, and glides without crashing to the ground. The answer might be surprising: It creates tiny tornadoes with its wings that keep it aloft.

When a dragonfly flaps its wings, the front edge of each wing slices through the air. This makes the air swirl around in a little spinning spiral, like a tiny, invisible tornado. These swirling mini tornadoes create low pressure above the wing, which helps pull the dragonfly upward and gives it extra lift. Because dragonflies have two sets of wings (front and back) that can beat together or separately, they can make these little tornadoes work in special ways, giving them excellent flying skills.

This feature of flight is called a ***leading-edge vortex***. Many insects, including bees, butterflies, flies, and sphinx moths, use leading-edge vortices to fly. This means they flap their wings in a way that creates extra lift.

Imagine all the insects flying around on a summer's day. Now picture all the tiny tornadoes they are creating in the air!

Before the invention of high-speed cameras, which helped scientists understand leading-edge vortices, insect flight remained a mystery. In the 1930s a French insect scientist (entomologist) named Antoine Magnan said that, using the math they had at the time, bumblebee flight seemed impossible. But we obviously see bees flying. With new technology and curious minds, we now understand how God carefully designed many insects, including dragonflies, to masterfully navigate the skies.

Time to Explore

Enjoy a morning near a pond and watch for dragonflies in flight. What directions do they fly in? Imagine a dragonfly receiving messages from its wings and adjusting flight to snag breakfast while in the air. Try drawing its flight pattern in a nature journal. If you see several dragonflies, make a record of how many you see and in what colors.

Possible by Design

Scientists were long puzzled by how insects, like dragonflies, stay in the air. Their bodies seemed too heavy for their wings to lift. And yet, with time, technology, and curiosity, they discovered God's detailed engineering. What once seemed impossible—dragonfly flight—was possible by God's design.

What in your life feels impossible? Can you trust that God has detailed plans you cannot yet see? Sometimes it's hard to believe in God's good plans. But we can trust that he is working out the problems we see and the ones we don't even know about. He already has answers to our questions, just as he always knew how he created dragonflies to fly.

Proverbs 16:9 reminds us, "We can make our plans, but the Lord determines our steps" (NLT). It is good to prayerfully make plans but to also hold those plans loosely. Like a dragonfly receiving information from its wing sensors and adjusting course, we should be open to a new direction as God gives us wisdom.

Jeremiah 29:11 reminds us, "'For I know the plans I have for you,' says the Lord. 'They are plans for good and not for disaster, to give you a future and a hope'" (NLT).

When something feels impossible, remember God is at work behind the scenes in every detail.

Dear God, thank you for designing dragonflies as amazing stunt flyers. We are so glad you led scientists to discover how you engineered this amazing creature. Help us to trust your design for our lives and to follow carefully as you guide us in your plans. Amen.

6

Canada Goose

Follow the Leader

Autumn's Song

What sounds remind you of autumn? Maybe it's the crackling of a campfire or the rustling of dry leaves as wind gusts shake them from the branches. Another familiar song of autumn is the honking of geese high overhead, signaling that summer has come to a close and winter is drawing near. Goose noises might not be as elegant as a songbird's chorus, but honking while flying helps geese succeed in their long migration journeys. Each spring, geese travel north to find nesting grounds to raise their young. In the fall, they fly south to warmer areas with more food. Geese honk while flying to communicate with one another. They might honk to warn each other of danger, or to stay together and in the correct formation. But why do geese line up in a V-shape as they fly across the sky?

Energy Efficient Flying

Geese need to travel a long way to find nesting grounds or food. By traveling together in a V, they can stay safe and save energy. The V formation is a type of ***echelon***, which refers to an arrangement of soldiers, ships, vehicles, or aircraft—or in this case, geese! An echelon of geese is an example of very smart aviation, or flight, as it saves energy for every goose except the leader. (Don't worry, we'll learn about the lead goose in a moment!)

When a goose flaps its wings to fly, it creates a slight rush of upward wind called an ***updraft***. The goose directly behind can ride the updraft, requiring it to do less flapping on its own. Each goose receives these small boosts of help from the goose in front of it.

The updraft boost builds like a wave as it works through the formation, becoming stronger, so that the two geese at the ends of the V formation receive the most benefit and have the easiest time flying.

The V formation also helps geese keep track of each other so they can stay safe with the flock. When I guide nature hikes with children, we have a safety rule that each child needs to be able to see our group at all times. No one should run ahead, fall behind, or wander off the trail alone. Geese practice a similar safety protocol by flying in V formation, so every goose is accounted for.

Who's the Leader?

If geese save energy by flying in the updraft of the goose in front of them, then how does the goose in the lead save energy? The goose in the front has the most challenging job, but it doesn't keep the same position for the entire journey. Instead, geese in the flock regularly swap out the lead position. When a lead goose needs rest, it slows down to go to the back of the formation, where it can fly more easily, while a different, well-rested goose can take the lead for a while.

Research suggests that by trading positions along the way, each goose shares a similar amount of responsibility and spends around the same amount of energy throughout the flight. Flying in this pattern can be about 70 percent more efficient than flying alone.

We can learn a lot from a flock of geese about sharing responsibility and working with others as a team.

Time to Explore

Watch for geese flying in a V formation. You can see this often in spring or autumn, when geese are migrating. If it's not migration season, look for geese foraging for food in fields or resting near water. Watch how they interact with each other, but don't join in, as geese can be very protective and aggressive.

Follow the Leader

Do you think of yourself as a leader? Have you ever led a game, taught someone something new, or helped a group follow instructions or carry out a plan? You might feel like a great leader, or you might be afraid to speak up and make your ideas known. Whether or not you feel strong in this area, God created you to be a leader. We all have opportunities to lead in different ways. You might lead in an obvious way, such as on a sports team. Or you might lead in a more unseen way, like teaching a younger sibling how to read or tie their shoes.

Watch for opportunities to lead, and when you see one, ask God to help you be a good leader. What do you think makes a good leader? Think about a goose leading the V formation. It is not looking for praise or fame. Instead, it is taking on a challenging role, giving its energy, and helping the geese behind it so the whole flock can be safe and successful. Similarly, God's design for leadership is not about seeking attention, but rather about serving others. Matthew 20:26 gives us a great picture of leadership: "Whoever wants to be a leader among you must be your servant" (NLT).

When Jesus lived on earth, he set an excellent example for us to follow. Mark 10:45 says, "For even the Son of Man came not to be served but to serve others and to give his life as a ransom for many" (NLT).

Jesus did not come to earth seeking fame. Instead, he came to serve us, and he went to the extreme of serving by giving his life for us so we can be with God forever. Thankfully, Jesus did not stay in the grave. Instead, he rose to life so that we also can have new, eternal life and can follow Jesus—the greatest leader—for all time. And do you know something amazing? When Jesus leads our life, he always remains at the front, guiding, protecting, and offering us rest as we trust and follow him.

Dear God, thank you for creating geese to fly in a V so they can stay safe and so we can learn about leadership. Help us to see opportunities to lead with your love. Help us to lead by serving others, not seeking attention for ourselves, but instead giving all praise to you. Amen.

7

Pitcher Plant

Choosing to Serve

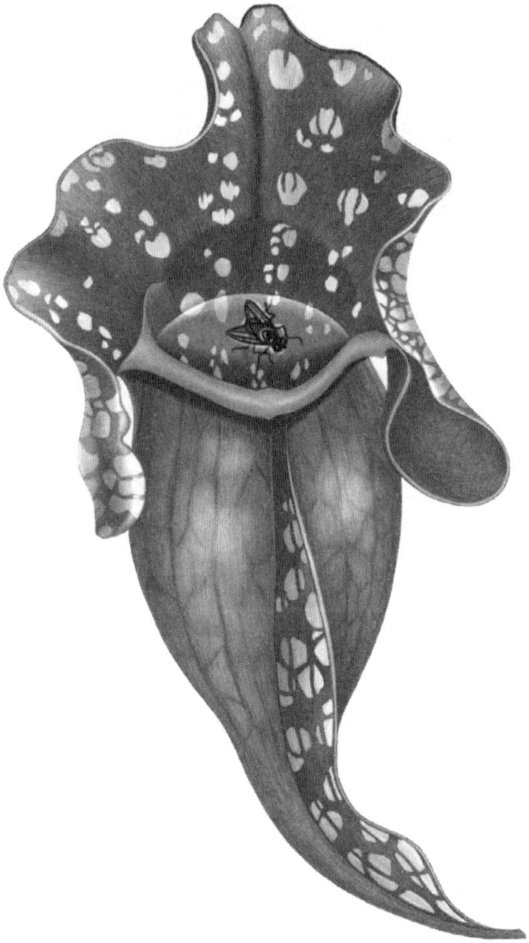

Insects on the Menu

We often think of insects eating plants, but what about plants eating insects? Perhaps you have heard of the Venus flytrap, which despite its name, is not from Venus. It's from North and South Carolina. The Venus flytrap is famous for its trick of trapping and digesting flies, but there are other types of plants that get their nutrients from insects; they are called ***carnivorous plants***.

Carnivorous plants do not eat in the same way that we do. They do not have mouths with tongues to taste or teeth to chew. They also don't have throats to swallow or stomachs to digest food. Instead, God designed them with ways to trap insects, and once they do, they use a special liquid with ***enzymes*** (specific proteins) to break down the insect's body and absorb or take in nutrients from that insect.

Although Venus flytraps grow naturally only in North and South Carolina, another carnivorous plant, the pitcher plant, is more widespread.

Like Venus flytraps, pitcher plants grow in bogs. A ***bog*** is a special ecosystem (natural area) that is very wet and has a springy floor made of living and decaying plants, mostly ***sphagnum moss***. This special moss is soft and squishy and holds a lot of water (like a sponge). It can grow on top of water, such as in lakes and ponds.

A bog has acidic soil with very few nutrients, making it impossible for most plants to grow there. But the plants that do grow in bogs are quite special. Carnivorous plants do well in bogs because they take nutrients from insects instead of relying only on the soil, which doesn't have much to offer them.

I once found pitcher plants in a bog in Wisconsin. They were easy to find, as their tall, single flowers stretched up high above the bog grasses, signaling like a flag to show where the pitcher plants were.

A Clever Design

How exactly does a pitcher plant trap insects? Unlike the Venus flytrap, it does not have leaflike structures that close when they are triggered by pressure (like a fly's footstep). Instead, true to its name, it has a pitcher-shaped leaf that holds liquid inside. It looks a bit like a pitcher holding lemonade on a hot summer's day.

The pitcher plant has sweet nectar on its rim, which entices insects to come visit. The rim is slippery, and insects often fall into the pitcher. The liquid inside is a mix of rainwater, enzymes, and microorganisms (tiny living things we need a microscope to see) that help break down insects. The pitcher also has small, hairlike structures that point down, making it nearly impossible for an insect to climb out once trapped inside. The digestive enzymes in the liquid begin to break down the insect, allowing the plant to absorb its nutrients, much like acids in your stomach break down food and help your body take in helpful nutrients from what you eat.

Helpful Pitchers

Although a pitcher plant means certain death for some insects, it is helpful to other creatures. Frogs in Borneo (a large island in Southeast Asia) turn the inside of pitcher plants into nurseries for their baby tadpoles. They lay their eggs in the pitcher plant's liquid, where their tadpoles hatch and are protected. The liquid does not harm them. The frogs have a safe place to raise their families, and the pitcher plant gets helpful nutrients from the frogs' droppings. This is called a ***mutualistic relationship***, which means that both living things benefit from each other.

Frogs are not the only creatures that help and receive help from pitcher plants. Another mutualistic relationship is between bats and pitcher plants. A species of bat in Borneo roosts inside the cozy pitcher plant, and when the bat poops, its droppings provide nutrients for the plant.

These are only two of many creatures that are helped by pitcher plants and offer something in return. These mutualistic relationships give us glimpses of how God meant for pitcher plants to operate in his perfect design.

Time to Explore

Go outside and look for nature participating in mutualistic relationships. Can you see an insect pollinating a flower? The insect receives sweet, nutrient-rich nectar, and the flower gets help spreading pollen. Or can you see an earthworm tunneling through the soil? The earthworm receives food, and the soil gets air and water, which helps plants grow better. Consider how God designed things in nature to support other living things. Can you draw a picture or write a short story about things in nature helping each other?

Choosing to Serve

God has given us many examples in nature of living things helping each other. Nature is connected through countless relationships, just as God's children depend on and serve one another in relationship. However, creatures and plants don't go out of their way to serve. Instead, as they go about their normal activities, other things in nature receive help, like how the pitcher plant provides a safe nursery for frogs. But God created people differently. We get to choose to serve those in our lives and around the world. We can go out of our way to serve even when it might be challenging or we receive nothing in return.

Jesus gave us the ultimate example of serving others when he gave up his life for us on the cross. John 15:13 says, "Greater love has no one than this: to lay down one's life for one's friends" (NIV). We will probably never find ourselves in a situation where we need to sacrifice our life for another person, but this verse reminds us that we should serve others even when it's hard. We can place the needs of others in front of our own wants.

Philippians 2:3–4 reminds us what should motivate us to serve: "When you do things, do not let selfishness or pride be your guide. Instead, be humble and give more honor to others than to yourselves. Do not be interested only in your own life, but be interested in the lives of others."

Dear God, it's so fun to see your plants and creatures working together. Help us to look for ways we can serve someone today and to help others even when it's hard. Thank you for serving us in the biggest way when you gave your Son to save us. Amen.

8

Earthworm

Unseen Work

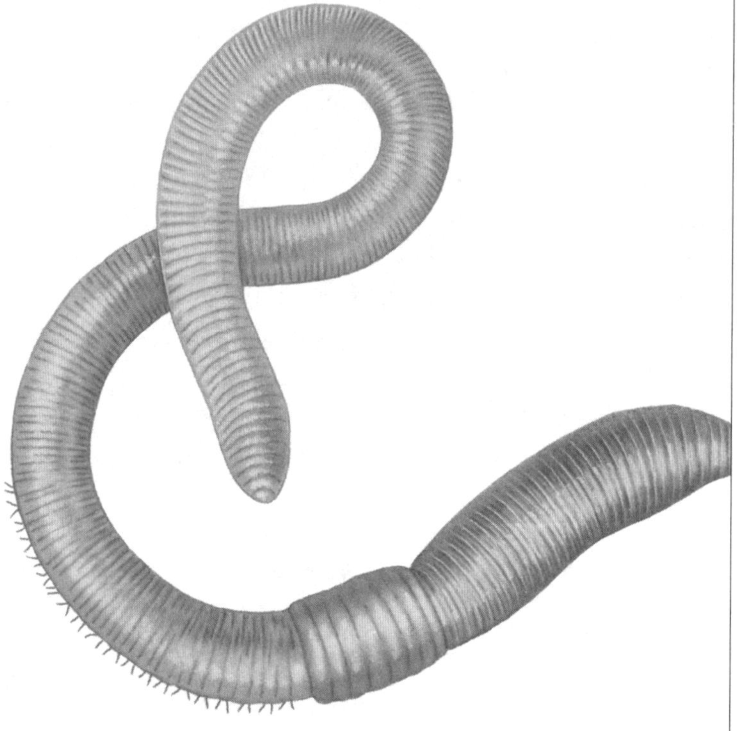

A Special Wriggly Design

Worms might seem like one of the simplest creatures around us. They don't have legs, arms, feet, or hands, so it might be difficult to tell their heads from their rear ends. Where are their eyes? Do they even have any? No, they do not. To make things stranger, earthworms don't even have bones. And yet God carefully engineered this eyeless, limbless creature to masterfully navigate and move through the underground world.

If you've ever held an earthworm or observed one closely, you may have noticed that it has stripes running around its body. These are called ***segments***, and they are part of an excellent design for contracting and expanding its body, helping the earthworm move through soil. Many of the segments have tiny bristlelike structures, almost like hair, called ***setae*** (pronounced SEE-tee) that further help a worm grip and move through soil. An earthworm, whose design can seem so simple, is an incredible reminder that God gives creatures exactly what they need to find their way, just as he carefully guides us through every circumstance we encounter.

Muscles for Bones

Have you ever watched a worm make its body longer and shorter? Maybe you have watched as one end of a worm stretches out long, then squeezes to make its body shorter and plumper. How exactly does a worm expand and contract its body? Beneath an earthworm's skin—by the way, it breathes through its skin!—are two sets of special muscles. The first set of circular muscles wraps around the earthworm, forming rings like the segments we see. The second set is underneath the circular muscles, running in the opposite direction—lengthwise from head to tail. A worm uses both sets to lengthen and shorten its body as it needs to.

These special muscles are called ***hydrostat muscles***, and they act as a skeleton, since the worm does not have bones. Hydrostat muscles provide a strong support system to creatures with no bones, such as octopuses, or certain parts of a creature with no bones, like an elephant's trunk. Hydrostat muscles use fluid and muscle to allow these creatures to move as if they had bones supporting them. An octopus can walk across the ocean bottom using the hydrostat muscles in its eight boneless arms. Although an elephant's trunk lacks bones, it can move like an extra arm by using over forty thousand hydrostat muscles in its trunk alone. (Compare that to the entire human body, which has around six hundred muscles.)

Maybe you have tried to grab a worm from the dirt only to have it cling to the ground on one end. Or perhaps you have watched a bird with one end of a worm in its beak, struggling to pluck it from the soil as the worm's body stretches out. The worm is trying to stay safe using its hydrostat muscles and bristlelike setae to cling to the ground. But why does the worm want to remain underground? What does it do beneath the soil all day?

Worker Worms

Maybe you have heard of worker bees, but have you ever heard of worker worms? God created worms as gardeners. One way gardeners and farmers help plants grow is by ***aerating*** the soil. When we use a shovel to dig up a layer of dirt and flip it over, air gets into the soil, which helps plants grow. Worms do this naturally as they wriggle through the dirt.

Earthworms aren't thinking about tilling the land. Instead, they are simply looking for their next meal. As an earthworm moves through the soil, it eats the dirt, along with other natural things like leaves and decaying sticks, and later the worm poops it out. This, too, is a carefully designed process. The earthworm digests the materials and takes the nutrients it needs, and the rest returns to the land as fertilizer. You can see these helpful poop piles, called ***castings***, next to holes where worms have burrowed beneath the ground.

Worms are to thank for the healthy, nutrient-rich soil found around plant roots just below the surface of the ground. The next time you see beautiful land with wildflowers, bushes, or trees, consider the not-so-simple worms beneath your feet helping to make it all happen.

Time to Explore

Go look for worms. Flip over logs and rocks to find worms of different lengths. Compare their sizes by gently laying them on paper and marking their measurements with a pencil. What is the largest worm you can find? When you carefully pick one up, does its body stretch out as it uses its muscles and setae to cling to the dirt? Place it in a bucket and see how it wriggles. Can you see the tiny bristlelike setae if you use a magnifying glass to look closer? Thank God for the excellent design of worms and how their daily activities grow beautiful plants for us to enjoy.

Unseen Work

Does it ever feel like no one sees your hard work? Perhaps you worked very hard on an art project, school assignment, or household task only to feel unappreciated. Maybe you felt like a worm working hard beneath the soil, with no one seeing your effort. Did you know that no matter who sees or does not see our work, God always does? He loves seeing you work hard to create beauty and help others.

It can be challenging to keep working hard if we don't receive thanks or a reward from other people. But Galatians 6:9 says, "We must not become tired of doing good. We will receive our harvest of eternal life at the right time if we do not give up."

When we work hard, we do not need to look for praise or thanks from others. Instead, we can know that God is pleased, and that is more than enough. In Matthew 6, Jesus talked about giving to others. In verse 4 he said, "Your giving should be done in secret. Your Father can see what is done in secret, and he will reward you."

Why don't you practice doing some unseen work today and take joy in knowing your efforts are seen by your heavenly Father? Consider cleaning something in your home or helping a neighbor or friend without them knowing it is you. Let them enjoy simply knowing someone was thinking of them.

Dear God, thank you for creating worms to mix up soil and make it easier for plants to grow. Even if our work goes unseen, we are grateful you see our efforts. We don't need to work to impress others or to be rewarded. You created us to do good works, and you delight when we work hard. Show us new ways to bless others. Amen.

9

Crow

Faithful Friendships

Problem-Solving Birds

Have you ever tried to open a walnut shell to get the nut inside? It's difficult, but humans have tools to open tough walnut shells. Crows, who eat walnuts, also face the challenge of opening their shells. They cannot walk into a store and purchase nuts already removed from their shells. Thankfully, God designed crows with brilliant brains, and they have been known to use their intelligence to solve many problems, including opening nuts.

In Tokyo, Japan, crows have been observed using cars to crack open walnuts for over thirty years. This is how it works: A crow collects a walnut from a nearby tree, then drops it on the road near a traffic stop. The crow waits for a car to drive over the walnut, cracking it open and breaking it into pieces. Then, when the traffic light changes and the cars stop, the crow safely swoops down and collects its snack.

Crows belong to a group of birds called ***Corvidae***, which also includes blue jays, magpies, and ravens. Birds in this category are smart. Along with understanding traffic patterns, crows have been seen solving puzzles, and they have excellent memory. Although it's hard for us to tell one individual crow from another, crows remember humans by their faces. If a human tries to harm a crow, the crow can remember that human for years afterward and knows to avoid them.

Crow Families Stick Together

Many types of birds leave their families shortly after learning to fly, but crow chicks are different. A young crow will stay with its family for an entire year after hatching, or sometimes longer. Crow families travel together so they can live with and learn from one another. You might find parent crows with their new young chicks, along with their chicks from the previous year.

If you have an older brother, sister, or cousin, they may have taught you a skill, like climbing a tree or catching a grasshopper before it leaps away. A crow that is a year old stays with its family to help raise and teach new chicks and also to continue to learn many life lessons from its parents. Crows have skills and behaviors that help them survive, and they take their time learning all they can from their parents before heading out on their own.

Tight-Knit Communities

God designed crows to enjoy company and to live well through community. They are not meant to be alone.

In fall and winter, when it is not breeding season, crows return every evening to a large roosting area. Here is how it works:

During the day, small groups of crows (often families) forage for food and help protect each other. Toward the end of the day, the small group begins traveling back to the roosting area. They use the same flight paths each day. As they travel, they rejoin other small groups of crows. You can often hear them "cawing" to each other. The smaller groups join up to become medium groups, which join up to become larger groups. Eventually, all these groups of crows arrive at the roosting area where they spend the night. A crow roost can have a few hundred to a few hundred thousand crows.

Crows understand they are safer when they are together with other crows. A group of crows (called a murder) is in less danger of being attacked by a predator. Young crows learn to rely on groups of crows and an entire community at a roosting site.

Time to Explore

Look for crows traveling together. Can you spot a group of a few crows? Could it be a family? Adult crows are shiny black. A crow that is one year old has more matte (not glossy) black feathers that fade to brownish in winter. If you think you see crow parents with their young, make up a story or song about their family.

If you see crows flying overhead at dusk, watch for a while to see if more follow. You might be watching a flight path the crows are using to return to their roosting area.

Faithful Friendships

Who do you spend the most time with? Who do you consider to be your closest friend or friends? Do you think the way they talk and behave affects how you act? Your friend may use a specific phrase that you have also started using. Or maybe your sister or cousin taught you how to play a game and then you taught it to your friend and they began playing that game with their family as well. This is called ***influence***. Influence is the way our actions or words can change how someone else thinks, feels, or acts. Influence is powerful, and the people closest to us often have the most significant influence (or impact) on our lives.

Think of how a crow family spends their days together. The parent crows have a lot of influence over their young chicks. One-year-old crows have influence over the newer chicks. Now picture a family of crows flying back toward their roost. They might stop partway for a snack and to join up with another family of crows. As they find food with the other family and fly some of the journey alongside them, one crow family might influence the other. Now picture the entire roost of thousands of crows. Do you think some of those crows are influencing others?

People are similar. The friends you spend the most time with shape your life. That's why it's so important to choose your closest friends wisely.

The Bible gives us good advice for growing faithful friendships. First Corinthians 15:33 says, "Bad friends will ruin good habits." And Proverbs 13:20 tells us, "Spend time with the wise and you will become wise, but the friends of fools will suffer."

So be like the crow that sticks with the right flock. Choose friends who love Jesus, help you grow in faith, and who you can encourage also. Together, you can help each other grow closer to God!

Dear God, we are so glad you made crows for community and to learn from each other. Thank you for the gift of friendship. Help us choose our closest friends well so we can cheer each other on in following you. Amen.

10

Crayfish

A Quick Getaway

Crayfish Babies

One spring afternoon, in the creek behind our home, my kids discovered a crayfish with eggs. They carefully picked up the crayfish mother and turned her over, revealing a clump of many tiny black orbs that were attached to the underside of her ***abdomen*** (the largest part of the crayfish's body, which looks like a tail). The orbs looked like clusters of tiny grapes without stems, but they were actually the crayfish's eggs. My children carefully returned the mother crayfish to the creek water, and we marveled at what they had found.

A mother crayfish normally lays eggs in spring and attaches them to her ***swimmerets***. Swimmerets are a special part of the crayfish's body that look like little feathers attached beneath its abdomen. The mother creates a sticky mucus that acts like glue, then she attaches her eggs to the swimmerets. This glue works very well, as the eggs remain attached to her underside for around five to eight weeks before hatching. A mother can lay around one hundred eggs. Some species can even lay a few hundred. That is a lot of eggs to have attached to her underside for up to two months!

Even after the baby crayfish hatch, they remain attached to their mother for a few days to a couple of weeks. Soon, they will begin venturing off in the water, but they still return to the safety of their mother's abdomen until they are ready to go off on their own.

A Complicated Build

What do you picture when you think about a crayfish? Although our attention is often drawn to its impressive front pincers, the crayfish has many other features that we can marvel at.

Crayfish use their two large pincers for grabbing and crushing food, defending themselves, mating, and building burrows. They also have smaller pincers on two sets of their walking legs. How many pincers does that make in total? Six! The smaller pincers help dig and grab and carry things.

God designed crayfish with more ways to navigate and find what they need in the freshwater lakes, ponds, rivers, streams, and marshes they call home. Two sets of antennae allow them to sense what is around them to find food. God also equipped them with two large compound eyes made of tiny lenses that are held up above their head on stalks. Each eye can move on its own, so a crayfish can look in two directions at one time as it searches for food or to spot and flee from something that might want to eat it for lunch.

What looks like the crayfish tail is its abdomen, which is made of six segments that are bendable and have strong muscles. The flexible abdomen helps the crayfish make quick getaways in the water. Because crayfish spend their lives in the water, God also equipped them with gills, which are under their bodies at the base of their walking legs. Like fish, they use their gills to breathe underwater.

Think about how God spoke the crayfish into creation. He fashioned its body plan with incredible and important details. God didn't have any do-overs or mistakes. He knew precisely what the crayfish would need and designed it just right to live in its underwater world and to raise its young.

Fleeing Dangerous Situations

A crayfish tail is engineered to help it make a quick getaway. The crayfish can swim backward very quickly and retreat to safety. But how does it flee so fast?

When playing a game of catch, have you ever placed your hands in front of your face to protect yourself when a ball came flying right toward you? Your brain saw the danger and told your body to respond. The crayfish can react much quicker to danger than we can.

Crayfish have a circuit system running through their bodies, which includes giant ***neurons*** that send messages to their brains. This circuit system can sound an alarm if a fish swims too close or if an animal casts a shadow over the water. Once the neurons send an alarm to the brain, the brain sends a message to tell the abdomen to do a move called the ***caridoid escape reaction***, or ***tail-flip***. This movement quickly shoots the crayfish backward and away from danger. While it might take us a few seconds to guard our face after seeing the threat of a ball, a crayfish can react to danger within twenty milliseconds (0.02 seconds) of sensing danger. That makes for a quick getaway!

Time to Explore

Do you have a freshwater pond, lake, river, or stream near you? With an adult, explore a shallow area of water and look for crayfish. They often hide under rocks. You can carefully lift rocks to check underneath. If you spot one, pay attention. Did it use its tail-flip move to quickly get away from you? If you decide to pick one up, be careful of its pincers and be gentle to not harm it. Turn the crayfish over. Can you see its swimmerets?

Imagine what it's like to see in two directions at one time, like a crayfish. Pretend to be a crayfish in the water and draw a picture of what you might see to both your left and right.

A Quick Getaway

Like a crayfish, we sometimes need to make a quick getaway. The Bible warns us against the dangers of sin and temptation in 2 Timothy 2:22: "But run away from the evil desires of youth. Try hard to live right and to have faith, love, and peace, together with those who trust in the Lord from pure hearts."

Have you ever heard of Joseph in the Bible? God used Joseph in many ways, and Joseph had to flee temptation and sin. In Genesis 39:12, when he had the opportunity to do something that went against God, he literally ran away from the situation.

Like a crayfish's specially designed tail helps it escape danger, God gives us what we need to flee the dangers of sin. First Corinthians 10:13 promises us this: "When you are tempted, he will also give you a way to escape so that you will be able to stand it." And do you know what happens as we practice making a quick getaway from sin? The enemy will start fleeing from us! James 4:7 says, "Submit yourselves, then, to God. Resist the devil, and he will flee from you" (NIV).

As we live by God's ways, the enemy will see God's power in us, and he will have to make a quick getaway.

Dear God, thank you for designing crayfish so wonderfully. You have given us all we need to flee sin and stay safe in your power. When we are tempted to do something that doesn't please you, help us to react quickly, retreating to the safety of your presence. Amen.

11

Loon

Finding Your Voice

Lake Life

At first glance, someone might think a loon is a duck, with its long, pointed body that glides across the surface of a lake. But a loon's colors are very different from a duck's. It is black and white with a magnificent, checkered pattern on its back and white striping on its chest, along with a white-striped band around its lower neck. The loon looks a bit like a duck wearing a fancy tuxedo.

God designed loons to be more comfortable on the water than in the air. While ducks and most other flying birds have light, hollow bones that help them fly, loons have heavier, solid bones that help them with their life in the water. Solid bones make a loon less buoyant, so it can easily plunge beneath the water. If you watch a loon, it might disappear right before your eyes. Many times I have called to my husband or children to come see a loon only to have it dive beneath the surface before they could catch a glimpse.

It is a good thing that God designed loons to dive well, because they rely on diving to catch the fish they eat. Loons can remain underwater for up to five minutes and dive up to two hundred feet deep. However, most dives are shorter and shallower. I love sitting at the edge of a lake and watching a loon dive, then guessing where it might resurface.

Seaplane Birds

When it's time to fly, loons must take off from the water instead of land. A loon's bones and body are too heavy for its wings to lift itself into the air like other birds. Also, its legs are positioned very far back beneath its body. Picture an airplane with its wheels placed nearly at the rear of the plane. This leg placement helps the loon with swimming, but it makes it impossible to take off from solid ground.

Instead, a loon is like a seaplane, which uses the water as its runway. A loon will run along the surface of the water, sometimes up to a quarter mile, and then fly straight into the wind. As it runs, it flaps its wings rapidly, catching the wind beneath them to lift its heavy body into the air. A loon requires a long water runway and can even become stuck if it lands on too small a pond.

If you have the chance to watch a loon gliding across the surface of a calm lake or diving below to catch fish before taking off into flight, you might agree that it seems much more at ease on the water than on land.

Yodeling Birds

Loons are most famous for the sounds and calls they make. A loon can sound like a coyote or wolf, which is fitting for its home on quiet, isolated lakes in the north. The male loon also makes an eerie yodeling song, mostly at dawn and dusk from spring to summer. If you hear a loon's yodel for the first time, your heart might beat more rapidly. It's an unfamiliar and striking, sometimes even unsettling, sound that echoes across the still waters of a lake.

Each male loon has a unique yodel, known as its ***voiceprint***. A loon's yodel has a specific tone, pitch, and timing. It is one of a kind, much like your fingerprint, which is unique to you. No other human has the same fingerprint.

However, a male loon's yodel can change over time. Yodeling is a territorial act for a loon. It yodels to proclaim a lake belongs to it so other male loons know not to come near. If a loon is chased off its lake and must relocate, its yodel might change, but it will still be unique to that individual bird.

Time to Explore

Go look for a bird swimming and diving. Along with loons, grebes and mergansers are types of waterfowl that dive. Watch one dive and point to where you think it might resurface. See if you're right! Count how many times a bird dives in ten minutes or use a stopwatch to time how long they're under the water.

Finding Your Voice

There are many birdsongs around a lake, but the loon's voice can be heard above them all. It is unique and beautiful.

You might feel at times like you have nothing special to say or as though your voice is drowned out by the noise of this world. This can be especially hard if you're a naturally quiet person. But just like a male loon, God created you with a unique voice and with special things to share with the world around you. Maybe you want to say, write, or sing something but think, *Why bother? Someone else can say it better.* Don't believe this lie. God created you with a unique story and way of communicating. Only you can share from your perspective.

The Bible shares the stories of several timid speakers. Have you ever heard the story of Moses? God called Moses to lead the Israelite people out of slavery and into God's promised land. When God told Moses to speak to Pharaoh on behalf of Israel, Moses replied in Exodus 6:30, "I am not a good speaker. The king will not listen to me." The New Living Translation says it this way: "I can't do it! I'm such a clumsy speaker! Why should Pharaoh listen to me?"

Yet God gave Moses the words and boldness he needed to approach Pharaoh and to lead the Israelites out of slavery.

Later, in 2 Corinthians 11:6, the apostle Paul said, "I may not be a trained speaker, but I do have knowledge." Paul was not trained in public speaking, yet he knew God's Word and ways, and he boldly shared them in his work as a missionary and in encouraging churches.

Whether you speak from a stage or share God's truth with a close friend or neighbor, God has given you a strong and unique voice. Don't believe the enemy's lies that might make you feel as though you have nothing important to say. You can speak courageously and confidently as you share God's words. If ever you are afraid to speak up, pray Acts 4:29: "Lord, help us, your servants, to speak your word without fear."

Like a loon's yodel, your voice might also change and grow over time. Moses's and Paul's voices matured as they saw God showing up in impossible situations. Past experiences and challenges will help you gain knowledge, and knowledge of God's Word will make your voice ever stronger.

Dear God, thank you for giving each of us a unique voice. Help us to use our voices to share your love and truth with others in exactly the way you created us to. May our voices always bring you praise. Amen.

12

Thistle

Making All Things New

Thorns and Thistles

Thistles are not the favorite plant of anyone I know. They are often associated with prickly thorns. Can you think of why? Both thistles and thorns begin with "th," and they are mentioned together in Genesis 3, right after Adam and Eve disobeyed God as part of sin's curse on creation.

> And to the man he said,
>
> > "Since you listened to your wife and ate from the tree
> >   whose fruit I commanded you not to eat,
> > the ground is cursed because of you.
> >   All your life you will struggle to scratch a living from it.
> > It will grow thorns and thistles for you,
> >   though you will eat of its grains." (vv. 17–18 NLT)

Sin's curse disrupted nature, and part of that brokenness is an overgrowth of thorns and thistles that make growing crops more difficult. Thorns, thistles, and similar plants are mentioned throughout Scripture and are often used as pictures of challenge, curse, and struggle. So, what exactly is a thistle, and do they serve a purpose?

What Makes a Thistle a Thistle?

Thistles are flowering plants in the same family as daisies and sunflowers (*Asteraceae*). However, thistles are marked with small spikes or prickles on their leaves and sometimes on their stems and at the base of flowers. A thistle's spikes act as a warning sign to animals that might want to eat it. They say, "Stay away, I'm spikey!"

A thistle's thorns help protect the plant, and they have also served as inspiration for humans. A related spikey plant in the same family, burdock, inspired a Swiss engineer named George de Mestral to invent Velcro in the 1940s. De Mestral noticed how spikey burs stubbornly attached to his dog's fur. When he placed the burs beneath a microscope, he noticed the tiny hook-and-loop mechanisms responsible for them sticking to clothes or fur. He used what he observed to invent Velcro, which humans use to secure things every day. Do you use Velcro anywhere in your home, such as on shoes, clothes, or a backpack?

Do Thistles Have a Place?

There are around two hundred types of thistles worldwide. Like any plant, thistles are most helpful if they grow where they belong. When a plant grows in its natural habitat, it is called a ***native plant***. When a plant grows where it does not belong, it is called an ***exotic plant***. Because of sin's curse, plants sometimes take over an area and leave little or no space for other plants. These are called ***invasive plants***.

Thorns and thistles remind us of sin's consequences. Because of sin, our relationship with God's creation is broken. Farmers, gardeners, and others who work the land have a challenging job keeping weeds, thorns, and thistles at bay. Invasive Canada thistles, which are native to Europe and Asia, plague farmers as they aggressively spread their roots, send up new plants, and take over pastures and land for growing crops. But it will not always be this way. As we'll see below, thistles are a beautiful reminder that God is making all things new.

Thistle Birds

Thistles growing in the wrong place—like a farmer's field—are a reminder of creation's brokenness, but they can also give us glimpses of God's grace.

Many creatures make good use of them. A thistle is a flowering plant, and its seeds, nectar, and pollen serve many creatures. Bees and other insects drink a thistle's sweet nectar for the nutrients they need.

Goldfinches rely on thistles so much that they are often called ***thistle birds***. Unlike many birds that feed insects to their chicks, goldfinches mainly feed their chicks seeds—mostly from thistles.

Thistles aren't used only as food but also for nesting. Their seeds have soft ***thistledown*** attached to them that catches on the wind to help the seeds spread. Goldfinches use the thistledown as a building material to cozy up their nests. They often build nests later in the season than other birds because they wait for the thistledown to be ready for them to use.

Time to Explore

Look for creatures using thistles. Thistles are a common roadside plant, so you can look along roads while driving or walking on the sidewalk. Can you see a goldfinch collecting seeds or soft down? Or a bee sipping on sweet nectar? Watch and remember that even thistles give us glimpses of God's grace as he cares for his creatures.

Use a book or, with permission, an online resource to learn about another plant that has a poor reputation (like a type of weed) and discover one way it serves a purpose in God's creation.

Making All Things New

Since before time began, God has had an incredible plan for those made in his likeness—a plan that no thistle or curse can get in the way of. First Peter 1:20–21 says, "Christ was chosen before the world was made, but he was shown to the world in these last times for your sake. Through Christ you believe in God, who raised Christ from the dead and gave him glory. So your faith and your hope are in God." Sin separates us from God, but Jesus restores hope and gives us a way back to our heavenly Father. Because of Jesus's death, burial, and resurrection, we can be made right with God and live with him in eternity.

Scripture also tells us that one day God will make all things new, sin's curse will be no more, and everything will be restored (Rev. 21:1, 5). This promise isn't only for the future. We can see hints of it here on earth. Psalm 104:30 says, "You make the land new again." Another translation says it like this: "You renew the face of the ground" (ESV). One day God will renew and restore his creation, and we'll get to see nature as he intended it, in perfect balance and harmony. That's how big God's grace is. As we wait for that day, we can remember God's goodness when we see a bee or a bird visiting a thistle, and we can know how God created everything with purpose.

In the garden of Eden, God promised to fix what sin had broken, and he fulfilled that promise through Jesus. Further, God is actively renewing the land and will one day make all things new. We have eternal hope, and even when things are hard and we don't understand, we can look to God's Word, enjoy his creation, and glimpse his grace even where it's least expected.

Dear God, thank you for using even a thistle to care for your creatures and for caring for your people even more deeply. When we see creatures using spikey thistle plants, remind us that you created everything with purpose and are making all things new. Amen.

13

Garter Snake

Splashes of Color

Snakes of Many Colors

Identifying a garter snake (often nicknamed a "gardener" snake) can be tricky. Even though the garter snake is a common snake to spot while exploring yards and neighborhoods, its colors and patterns can be puzzling. The reason for this is that God painted many unique designs on garter snakes. The garter snakes my siblings and I found and played with where we grew up in Wisconsin look very different from the garter snakes my kids and I discover in Colorado.

There are over four thousand snake species worldwide. About thirty-five of them are garter snakes—all in the genus ***Thamnophis***—and they're common across North and Central America.

God arrayed some species of garter snakes in yellow and brown and others in red, black, and blue. Most have stripes, and some have checkered patterns. A typical pattern on garter snakes is three stripes running down the body from the neck to the tail. In some species, these stripes are very easy to see, such as a black garter snake with white or blue stripes. Other garter snakes can have a brown body with more hidden yellow or olive stripes, making them great at hide-and-seek amid dirt and grass.

Even in the same species, individual garter snakes can look different. They remind us of God's creativity painted across many habitats.

Baby Garter Snakes

Recently, while playing at the river, my kids discovered a baby garter snake that was mostly brown with three lighter, sand-colored stripes. One stripe ran down the center of its back and the other two on each side, and it also had a black head. They named it Bite, although thankfully, it did not live up to its name. They enjoyed holding it and studying its movements before carefully placing it back into its habitat by the river.

We often think about snakes laying eggs, as they are reptiles, but garter snakes have their babies differently. Garter snakes are ***ovoviviparous*** (pronounced oh-voh-vih-VIP-er-us). This means they give birth in a special way that is a mix of both egg laying and live birth. The baby snakes (called ***snakelets***) grow inside eggs, but the eggs stay inside the mother's body instead of being laid outside, like in a nest. This means the baby garter snakes have extra protection—an egg and their mother's body wrapped around them! The babies come out of their mother in a thin ***membrane***. This membrane is kind of like a soft, stretchy bag that protects the babies.

A mother garter snake will typically have ten to forty snakelets. The small snakelets come out of their mother all curled up around themselves and look like a snake knot. After a few moments, they wiggle and break through the membrane so they can breathe and slither away on their own.

God designed garter snake babies to be able to move and find food right away, so they do not stick around with their mother. Instead, they begin venturing off to find what they need right from the start. That's what the baby garter snake was doing when my children discovered it. When they set it back safely in the brush, it slithered off to find its next meal.

Smelling with Tongues

As my children held the garter snake, it kept rapidly sticking its tongue out. We could see that the tongue was bright red. At its tip, the tongue forked into two points, which were jet-black. Have you ever seen a snake sticking out its tongue? It is not being rude. It is also not preparing to bite. Sticking out its tongue is how it learns about the world around it.

Snakes use their tongues to smell in a different way than we do. Their tongues collect tiny scent particles, like little packets of smells. Then they pull their tongue back into their mouth and press it against a special organ called the ***Jacobson's organ***, which sends messages to their brain to help them "smell" what's around them!

Time to Explore

Go find a garter snake in the wild or visit a reptile house or the zoo to see a snake up close. Never approach or touch a snake unless you are with a parent or trusted adult and you're certain it does not have venom. It's also wise to research if there are venomous snakes where you live, and if so, how to identify them.

Watch a snake as it moves across the ground or in the water. Can you see it sticking its tongue out to collect scent particles? What do you think it is smelling?

Ask a trusted adult to help you find a video online of a garter snake giving birth. Can you see when the small snakelets break free from the membrane?

Splashes of Color

Just as God painted garter snakes in many colors and patterns, he displays his creativity in human beings. Across the world, God showcases his beauty in creating humans with different skin tones, hair and eye color, and body shapes and sizes. We can delight in God's creativity as we appreciate the many ways he made humans.

While different species and even individual garter snakes can look very different from one another, they all belong to the *Thamnophis* genus. Similarly, humans can look very different from one another, but we are all made in the image of God.

Genesis 1:27 says, "So God created human beings in his image. In the image of God he created them. He created them male and female."

Do you think a garter snake with yellow coloring is jealous of a garter snake with black coloring and blue stripes? Or do you think a garter snake with stripes wishes it had a checkered pattern? Of course not. We do not need to wish we looked like someone else either. Psalm 139:14 says, "I praise you because I am fearfully and wonderfully made; your works are wonderful, I know that full well" (NIV).

Whenever you see a garter snake, delight in the unique colors and patterns God used to paint it and let it remind you that every human being, including you, showcases God's creativity and beauty.

Dear God, thank you for displaying your creativity in nature. Thank you for using many colors and patterns to wow us. We are so grateful you made humans special in your image and that we can enjoy all the wonderful things you've made. Amen.

14
Frog
Defeating Death

A Frog's Winter Nap

Do you ever wonder where frogs go when it gets cold outside? Frogs hatch from eggs in the water during spring. After the frog babies (called tadpoles) grow legs, they come up onto land. Many types of frogs take two to three years before they will head back to the water to breed and lay their own eggs. But what do they do when winter rolls around?

When temperatures drop, frogs take a long winter nap. God designed frogs and other amphibians, as well as reptiles, to survive cold temperatures by resting their bodies through a process called ***brumation***. Brumation is similar to the hibernation period some small mammals partake in, but it's a little different.

Mammals that hibernate are usually completely inactive during that time. In comparison, during brumation a reptile or amphibian, such as a frog, might wake up occasionally to take a drink. But they are very sluggish, they move slowly, and their bodies have slowed their internal processes. Their heart rate, their breathing, and their ***metabolism***—the body's process for breaking down food and turning it into energy—also slow to save energy.

Freezing Solid

One species of frog takes its winter nap very seriously: the wood frog. Wood frogs are commonly found throughout North America. They can live in the south, where it stays warm year-round, but they can also live up north in Alaska and Canada, including some Arctic regions, where they survive below freezing temperatures.

Wood frogs survive temperatures as low as 0.4 degrees Fahrenheit (-17.5 degrees Celsius)! The world around can freeze solid, and so can they.

Wood frogs enter a state called ***suspended animation***. When they do this, they are basically on pause from life. Their brain activity and heart rate stop. They are no longer breathing. By all appearances, they are no longer living. And yet, when spring rolls around and the land thaws, so do they. Their heart begins to beat slowly, and their brain wakes back up. The wood frog's body gradually begins working again until it completely thaws and resumes life as usual. But how exactly does its body survive freezing solid?

Nature's Antifreeze

Has a parent or adult you know ever poured antifreeze in their car? I grew up in Wisconsin, where it gets very cold in winter. To protect our cars' engines, my dad would add a liquid called antifreeze to the cars to keep them from freezing completely.

God engineered wood frogs and other creatures that freeze solid with the ability to produce natural antifreeze in their bodies.

They pump water out of their organs—the important parts of their bodies with special jobs to do. The water that leaves their organs turns to ice around them. They use ***glucose***, a type of sugar, to protect the organs from completely freezing. Why does this work? Sugar water freezes more slowly than pure water. You can test this by mixing sugar into a cup of water and placing it in your freezer next to a cup of pure water. Check back often and watch the pure water freeze solid before the sugar water does.

A wood frog appears like a little block of ice, but inside, its most important organs are safe and ready to return to regular activities when spring returns!

Time to Explore

Can you find a frog? If it's spring or early summer, you might be able to spot tadpoles swimming around a pond or lake's edge. If it's late summer, frogs might be hopping around wet areas or poking their eyes up above the water's surface. Once you spot a frog, gently catch it with your hands or a net. Can you count the toes on its front hands and back feet? Do you notice special patterns or colors on the frog? Once you're done observing it, carefully release it where you found it.

If it's fall or winter, frogs might be resting beneath mud or under logs or leaves. Leave them be—they need their rest!

Defeating Death

God designed wood frogs to avoid freezing to death by protecting their organs with antifreeze. They might look dead as they are frozen solid, but they can keep living when the land warms up.

Unlike a wood frog that looks dead but is still alive, Jesus actually died for us, and three days later, he rose to new life so we can enjoy eternal life in God's presence. Romans 5:8–9 says, "But God showed his great love for us by sending Christ to die for us while we were still sinners. And since we have been made right in God's sight by the blood of Christ, he will certainly save us from God's condemnation" (NLT).

Picture Jesus in the tomb after he died on the cross. Some people thought Jesus might have only fainted and was not truly dead, which would mean he didn't come *back* to life but instead just woke back up. But the Bible tells us Jesus truly did die. He was not in a coma or in a state of suspended animation. This is important because fainting would not have been enough to cover our sins. Jesus was the only perfect sacrifice able to bring us back to God.

First Peter 3:18 says, "Christ himself suffered for sins once. He was not guilty, but he suffered for those who are guilty to bring you to God. His body was killed, but he was made alive in the spirit."

Wood frogs might look like they have a trick to defy death, but they do not. Jesus, however, defeated death by rising from the dead in bodily form in order to rescue us from sin's penalty so we can live with God forever.

Dear God, thank you for designing frogs with the ability to protect their organs and live through harsh temperatures so we can marvel at their joyful hopping throughout summer. And thank you for sending Jesus to defeat death on the cross so we can know, follow, and be with you in eternity. Amen.

15

Raccoon

Let Your Eyes Shine

Masked Bandits or Helpful Pest Control?

Raccoons have a bad reputation for being masked bandits. They are dressed, of course, with a beautiful black eye mask across their face. But calling them bandits can be misleading. Although raccoons can get into trash cans or even steal eggs from a chicken coop, they spend most of their time controlling pest populations, which helps homeowners, gardeners, and farmers.

When raccoons are around, it's best to keep trash cans put away to discourage them from causing messy trouble and eating things that can harm them. When human trash is not an easy option, raccoons eat their natural diet, which includes berries and other fruits, seeds and nuts, amphibians, earthworms, small mammals and fish, and many insects. When raccoons find food, they sometimes do something very interesting before enjoying a meal—they wet it.

A Washful Habit

Can you think of any animals that are named for how they behave? Flying squirrels don't actually fly but are named after their flight-like free falls. Woodpeckers are named for their habit of pecking on wood to find insects, to communicate, or to create homes.

Raccoons are also named for their behavior. The raccoon's scientific name is ***Procyon lotor***. The word *lotor* means "washer." Raccoons are known for dunking their food in water before eating it, but why do they do this?

Perhaps when your family buys berries or lettuce at the grocery store, you wash them before eating to rinse off any dirt or possible bacteria. This is not why raccoons wash their food. It was long thought that raccoons cared about having a clean snack, but they are more concerned with the feel of their food. God designed a raccoon's front feet to be extra sensitive. A raccoon's front paws have many sensors that send messages to its brain about what it is feeling.

Just as we might smell food before we eat it, a raccoon feels its food with its paws to gather more information and make sure it is safe to eat. When a raccoon dips its food into the water, it kind of wakes up those sensors on its paws and helps it feel the details of its food even better.

In a way, a raccoon's paws help it "see" what it is holding, especially if it's dark.

Speaking of nighttime, raccoons are ***nocturnal*** navigators, which means they are mostly active at night. God designed them with super-sensor hands to help them stay safe and find what they need at night. He also gave them special eyes to see in the dark.

Glowing Eyes

Have you ever seen the glowing eyes of a raccoon in the dark? A raccoon's eyes do not actually glow. Instead, they reflect. Raccoons, along with most mammals, have a reflective layer (like a mirror) in the back of their eye. This layer is called a ***tapetum lucidum*** (pronounced tuh-PEE-tum LOO-sih-dum). Many animals that are active in low lighting, such as at dawn, dusk, or night, have this important mirror-like layer in their eyes that helps them see well. But how does it work?

Even at night, there's a little bit of light from things like the moon or city lights. A small amount of this light enters the raccoon's eye and bounces off the special tapetum lucidum mirror. When the light reflects, it travels back through the eye. This lets the raccoon "see" the light twice, which gives it extra illumination to see in the dark.

Time to Explore

How many animals can you name that are active mostly during the night?

Ask a parent or trusted adult to take you on an evening walk to see if you can spot an animal with a tapetum lucidum in their eyes. They can often be seen when a flashlight shines toward them after the sun has set or before it rises. Other common wild animals with reflective eyes are foxes, coyotes, cats, skunks, and deer.

Let Your Eyes Shine

A raccoon's eyes look like they glow at night, but they are only reflecting light directed toward the raccoon, such as light from a flashlight or car headlights. Its eyes do not create any light on their own.

Similarly, we do not create light, but we can reflect God's light so that others can see him at work in our lives. Psalm 19:8 says, "The commands of the LORD are radiant, giving light to the eyes" (NIV). God's truth, found in the Bible, gives light to our eyes, helping us clearly see how to follow him and live in his ways. Like light reflecting in a raccoon's eye, God's light of truth helps us see even in dark circumstances when life is difficult. When we are overwhelmed by darkness around us, we can go to God's Word. Psalm 119:130 tells us, "The teaching of your word gives light" (NLT).

A raccoon's eyes shine only when light is directed toward them. In the same way, as we turn our eyes toward Jesus, we don't only see his light but we also reflect it to those around us. When others look into our eyes, may they see the love of Christ shining back toward them.

Dear God, thank you for helping raccoons find what they need at night with their super-sensor hands and reflective eyes. Help us to keep our gaze fixed on you so we can reflect your light to the world around us. Amen.

16

Ant

Super Strength

Marvelous Ants

Have you ever watched ants go about their day? Maybe you stopped walking on a trail when you noticed ants filing in and out of a mound of dirt. Or perhaps you spotted a line of ants carrying crumbs back to their nests. Did your curiosity cause you to pause and wonder what these tiny creatures were up to? I once read this about watching ants: "I am sure that none of us can sit down by an ant nest and watch its citizens come and go, without discovering things that make us marvel."*

Remember, marvel means something causes great wonder, which can remind us to "stop and consider God's wonders" (Job 37:14 NIV).

When you stop to watch ants, you can notice how God created them with the knowledge of how to protect themselves and care for their ***colony***. Ants work together to care for their colony, and there is a lot of work to be done! As the queen ant lays eggs, the worker ants take care of all the ant nest business. Worker ants forage, going out to find food and bring it back for the colony. Nurse ants tend to the eggs and the baby ants, called larvae. Other worker ants are builders, and their job is to dig tunnels and expand the underground ant nest. Still other worker ants act as guards, protecting the entrances of the ant nest from intruders. There are also soldier ants that attack and fight off predators to the colony.

An ant nest is a busy place full of smart and efficient ants. As we watch them, we can glimpse God's wisdom and reflect on what Psalm 104:24 says:

> How many are your works, LORD!
> In wisdom you made them all;
> the earth is full of your creatures. (NIV)

Ants on the Move

My family recently saw ants marching in a long line, each ant carrying something in its mouth. We thought at first that they had found food and were carrying crumbs back to their nest. But what they carried all looked the same shape, size, and color. How could crumbs be so perfect?

* Anna Botsford Comstock, *Handbook of Nature Study* (Comstock Publishing Associates, 1986), 369.

Looking closer, we realized the ants were not carrying food crumbs but ant eggs! The ant colony was making a big move to a new nest site.

Ant colonies will relocate quite often, especially if their nest is disturbed by too much rainfall, conditions that are too dry, or too much human activity. When ants move to a new place, the worker ants start digging right away. In only a day or two, they can make enough tunnels for the queen and the colony to be safe. Then, little by little, they keep adding more tunnels and rooms for the growing colony.

When ants relocate, they move all the eggs with them, carrying them one by one. This is impressive to see, because an ant's egg cannot fit in its hand like we might hold an egg from a bird. Ant eggs can be nearly as large as an adult ant. Yet they work hard to move every egg to a new safe location. But how do they organize all this work?

Ants work well together because God designed them with ways to ***communicate***, or share information. Ants don't talk with words like we do. Instead, they communicate using smells. Their two antennae are covered in tiny, hairlike structures called ***sensilla***. These hairs help the ants smell and feel everything around them. Ants use their antennae to find their way home, follow scent trails, and recognize other ants. It's like their built-in super-sensor for exploring and communicating. With these amazing antennae, ants can find food and return with it, warn other ants of danger, avoid getting lost, and work together as a colony just as God designed.

Ant Power

Whether ants are carrying food crumbs back to the nest or carrying eggs to a new nest location, they have incredible strength! If you've ever watched an ant carrying something, you might have noticed it can carry things larger and heavier than itself.

That's because ants can lift and carry things ten to fifty times heavier than their own weight. That's like you picking up a whole car. God designed ants' small, compact bodies with strong muscles and a hard exoskeleton (or outer shell) to carry big loads and protect their colony. Their bodies are built just right to lift heavy things, move quickly, and even survive great pressure without getting squished.

Time to Explore

Watch ants at work. Proverbs 6:6–8 says we can become wiser by watching ants. Find an ant nest and carefully observe it. What are the ants doing? Do you see forager ants returning with food? Can you identify guard ants protecting the nest entrances? What lessons can you learn from them? Write a short story about ants working together and what they might be communicating to each other through smells. Then share it with your friends and family.

Super Strength

Whenever I watch an ant using its super strength, I'm reminded of the incredible power inside those who follow God.

God gave ants super strength for their work, and he gives us a different kind of super strength for the tasks he's created us for. Ephesians 1:19–20 says the power inside us is the same power God used to raise Jesus from the dead. That's incredible strength!

Imagine that kind of power working inside us and through us. Ephesians 3:20 says, "With God's power working in us, God can do much, much more than anything we can ask or imagine."

This doesn't mean we can fly like birds or carry cars, but God's power shows up in us in other ways—helping us to be brave, kind, forgiving, or strong when we feel weak. And we will at times feel weak and wonder where God's super strength is. However, when we feel weak, we can see God's strength shine. In 2 Corinthians 12:9, the apostle Paul reflected on God's words to him. "My grace is enough for you. When you are weak, my power is made perfect in you." In response to this promise, Paul wrote, "So I am very happy to brag about my weaknesses. Then Christ's power can live in me."

Instead of trying to be strong yourself, you can lean on God's power. Just as you might use a magnifying glass to look closely at ants, watch carefully to see God in the details of your life as he uses his power to give you strength just when you need it.

Dear God, thank you for designing ants with super strength and for using your incredible power in our lives. Help us to live by your strength each day. Amen.

17

Rabbit

Aware and Ready

A Rabbit Is Not a Rodent, So What Is It?

Have you ever been mistaken for someone else? This happens to rabbits often! Rabbits are mistaken for rodents that are similar to squirrels, mice, and rats. They were once classified as rodents, but in 1912, they were reclassified into a different order called ***Lagomorpha***. They are distinct and set apart from rodents for two reasons. First, they have two special teeth located directly behind their front teeth. Second, they cannot turn their front paws inward to grasp objects like squirrels or mice can. Rabbits are unique and magnificent creatures that God has made special in many ways. There is good reason to be curious about them, but we're not the only ones who are curious about these creatures. Many predators are too.

Always on the Run

Rabbits are a favorite meal of many animals, including foxes, coyotes, wolves, dogs, house cats, and hawks. They provide essential food for many creatures. And yet, even though many are hunted, rabbits flourish. I'm always surprised by how many rabbits I spot on a walk around my neighborhood. One reason they do well is because they have lots of babies.

Different conditions affect how many babies a mother rabbit can have—from very few to a lot. In general, a mother rabbit may have three to four litters each year, with three to eight babies in each litter. Can you do the math to find out how many babies a rabbit might have in a year? A mother could have as few as nine babies (three litters of three babies). Or she could possibly have as many as thirty-two babies (four litters of eight babies)! All those rabbits look very tasty to many creatures. And yet, not all of them end up as dinner. Come winter, when that year's babies have grown up and are out exploring and finding food, I see many rabbit tracks through the snow, offering hints as to what a rabbit has been up to that day.

With so many enemies, how do rabbits survive?

Home Sweet Home

A rabbit has a ***home territory*** of around two to seven acres. The rabbit uses a scent from a small gland, kind of like a pocket under its chin, to leave its unique smell around its territory.

Do you have a favorite grassy spot to sit in your yard? Rabbits do! A rabbit has not only soft grassy spots called ***forms*** but also crisscross trails and refuges inside bushes.

Rabbits are familiar with every inch of their territory, so they can use it to find food and shelter. I have seen this in action when a fox or neighborhood cat chases a rabbit through a yard. A rabbit knows the best route for a quick escape.

Sensing Danger

Rabbits have many ways of sensing danger. Their large eyes, positioned on the sides of their head, help them see what is going on around them. And have you ever seen a rabbit's nose twitching? That means it is smelling its surroundings. Humans rarely use smell to stay safe, except in cases such as smelling food that has spoiled or smoke from a fire. But God knew rabbits would need super smelling powers to stay safe, so he equipped them with a nose full of ***olfactory sensors***. These little sensors pick up smells and send information to the rabbit's brain.

Humans have around five to six million olfactory sensors, while rabbits have around one hundred million. They can detect a scent and figure out what it is twenty times better than we can.

Rabbits don't use only their eyes and noses to stay safe. They can also swivel their large ears, moving them in different ways at the same time to hear from multiple directions. When danger is around, a rabbit might freeze in place like a statue to remain unnoticed, or if a predator has found it, it will use its strong back legs to quickly leap away, following the well-known routes of its home territory to retreat to a safe place of refuge.

Time to Explore

Walk around your neighborhood in the early morning and try to find rabbits. They are active in the early morning when grass and other plants are often covered in fresh dew drops, which provide them with both food and water at the same time. Maybe walk the same route a few days in a row and chart how many rabbits you see each day. Do they appear in the same places? Perhaps you have found a rabbit's home territory and can find one of its favorite grassy spots to sit and rest.

Aware and Ready

Just as a rabbit must stay alert to danger, Scripture says we have an enemy that we need to keep aware of. First Peter 5:8 says, "Stay alert! Watch out for your great enemy, the devil. He prowls around like a roaring lion, looking for someone to devour" (NLT).

Thankfully, just as God equipped rabbits with incredible senses, God makes us aware of our enemy, the devil. God's Holy Spirit inside us can help us sense when the enemy is trying to trick us or trap us or lead us away from God's will and ways.

When we sense danger from the enemy, whether it's a wrong thought, a hurtful habit, or a sinful behavior, we can run to God for safety and help. After all, Proverbs 18:10 tells us, "The name of the LORD is a strong fortress; the godly run to him and are safe" (NLT). We become familiar with a clear, quick course back to God by studying and memorizing his Word, the Bible, and through praying.

When you see a rabbit twitching its nose, swiveling its ears, or running to safety, remember that God is "our refuge and strength, an ever-present help in trouble" (Ps. 46:1 NIV). He helps us stay aware of our surroundings and shows us a path to his safety.

Dear God, thank you for creating rabbits to stay safe so we can enjoy watching them. We are grateful that you are always with us. Help us to stay aware of any danger and troubles and to practice coming to you each day in your Word and through prayer. Amen.

18

Daddy Longlegs

Getting to the Truth

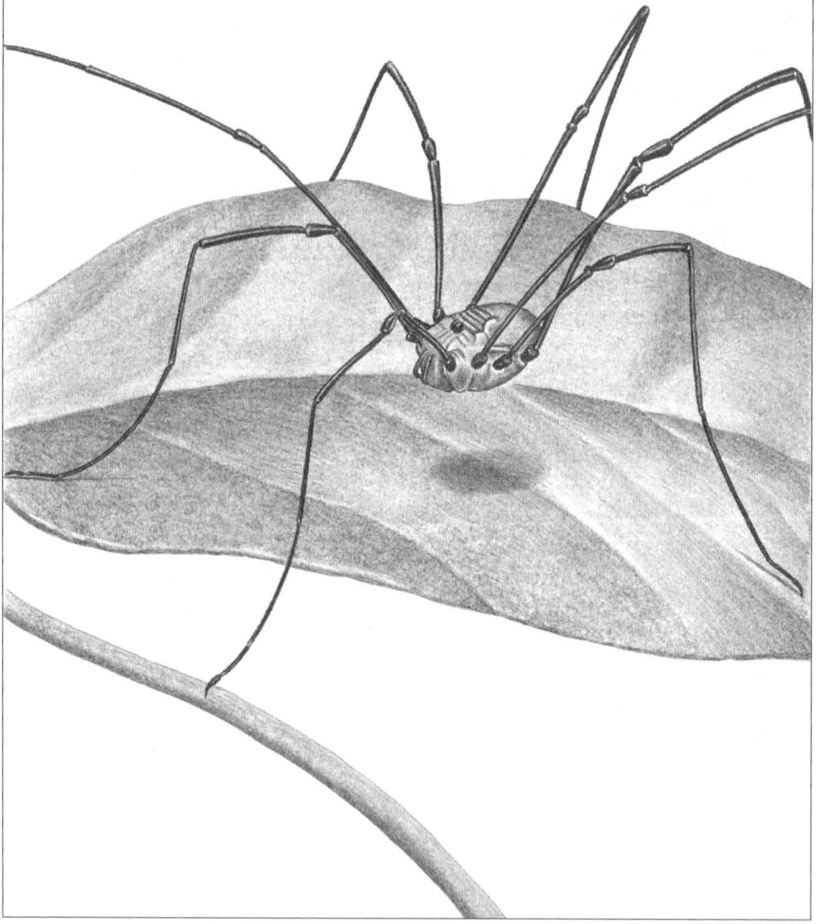

Mistaken Identity

Do you enjoy finding clues and piecing together mysteries? We have the chance to do that with a commonly misunderstood creature: the daddy longlegs. Daddy longlegs are often confused with spiders and for good reason: They look like spiders with their many long legs. However, they are not spiders. They are in the ***Arachnida*** class, along with spiders and scorpions. But when we zoom in closer, daddy longlegs are unique creatures that God designed differently from spiders.

If we look to the next level of taxonomy, spiders are in the ***Araneae*** order, and daddy longlegs are in the ***Opiliones*** order. These are a lot of big, science-y words, but what's important to know is this: Humans sort living things into categories to better understand what creatures are and are not. When sorting spiders and daddy longlegs, scientists put them into two different categories because of the ways God designed them uniquely.

One big difference between a spider and a daddy longlegs is that spiders have two main body parts: an abdomen and a ***cephalothorax***. But daddy longlegs have only one large, round body from which their eight legs extend. Another big difference is that daddy longlegs do not produce silk like spiders do.

A Poisonous Myth

When I was a child, I heard that daddy longlegs had the most potent poison of all spiders but that their fangs were not strong enough to pierce human skin. Many of my friends and I shared this belief. It felt courageous to handle the most poisonous spider in the world when one of us dared to hold one. Some children chose not to, whether they found the creature's long legs creepy or were afraid its fangs might have defied the odds and become strong enough to inject them with a deadly poison. Now I understand this is not accurate.

It was not until I was an adult that I learned the truth. First, as we've already learned, daddy longlegs are not spiders at all. Second, they have no venom and, in fact, no fangs. Daddy longlegs have a unique mouthpart called a ***stomotheca*** (pronounced stow-moe-THEE-ca). The stomotheca is not like a spider's fangs. Instead, it acts more like a crab's mouth and is designed for crushing and chewing solid food.

The part of the myth about a daddy longlegs not being strong enough to bite through human skin is actually true. They can't bite us, and even if they could, they do not have venom to hurt us.

It's important in nature study and every area of life to not simply believe everything we're told. God created us with curious minds for a reason, and we can let our curiosity guide us as we search out truth and dispel myths.

Time to Explore

Can you find a daddy longlegs? Can you tell if it's truly a daddy longlegs or a spider? Count the center body part, or parts, to see. If there's only one part, it's a daddy longlegs, but if there are two parts, it's a spider. If you find a daddy longlegs, be gentle with it and never pick it up by the leg. Their legs can detach and, contrary to another myth about daddy longlegs, they cannot grow them back.

Getting to the Truth

My friends and I were not in any danger as we held daddy longlegs, despite what we believed about them having venom. But what if the situation were different? Consider if someone told you a true spider with venom was harmless and you believed them. Nature reminds us that we should not believe everything we are told. Instead, God gives us something called ***discernment***, which helps us tell what is right and true from what is wrong or false.

First John 4:1 says, "Dear friends, do not believe everyone who claims to speak by the Spirit. You must test them to see if the spirit they have comes from God. For there are many false prophets in the world" (NLT).

What do you think it means that "there are many false prophets in the world"? This verse reminds us that many people who do not follow God, and do not have his Holy Spirit inside them, will try to trick us into believing Satan's lies. We need to practice identifying God's truth. How can we do that? We can

- read the Bible every day;
- study Scripture;

- memorize Bible verses; and
- make sure what we hear lines up with what God says in his Word.

As you become more familiar with God's Word, God's Spirit will help you discern truth from lies. John 16:13 says God's Spirit "will lead you into all truth."

A great and fun way to practice discernment is to begin noticing the details in nature. Look closely, research, and see what things are and what they are not, like how a daddy longlegs is different from a spider. Practice questioning what you hear and getting to the truth of what God has created.

Dear God, we are so glad you made daddy longlegs unique and special. Thank you for your truth, which shines brighter and stands stronger than any lies. Help us to practice seeing and discerning truth in nature and every area of life. Amen.

19
Vulture
A Clean Heart

Roadkill on the Menu

Have you ever seen a large bird flying right over the treetops? Some birds do this when searching for ***carrion***, the decaying flesh of dead animals. Vultures are well-known for feeding on animals that have recently died, such as roadkill. These animals who search for carrion are ***scavengers***, meaning they eat already dead animals rather than hunting live prey.

When we think about birds eating, we often picture a robin slurping up a worm or a songbird plucking berries from a bush. A vulture's meal is a bit messier and less pleasing to think about. But as we'll soon see, the eating habits of vultures are very important in nature.

God designed all birds with acids in their stomachs. These acids help break down the food they eat into nutrients their bodies use to grow stronger and stay healthy. Our bodies are engineered similarly. But a vulture needs extra-strong stomach acids to break down its tough diet of meat and even bones. Yes, some vultures eat bones! They don't have steak knives like humans use to cut meat from the bone, and some species, such as the bearded vulture, dine on their meal bones and all.

This seems gross to us, but the vulture's diet is essential for keeping God's creation clean.

Nature's Cleanup Crew

Have you ever seen an animal that was unfortunately hit by a car while trying to cross the road? It is sad to see, and it would be even harder if the animal was left on the road or beside it for a long time. It's not only sad to witness an animal that's been hit, but its continued presence is also dangerous to other creatures and us. Harmful bacteria can grow on dead animals, and diseases can spread from them. If other animals eat roadkill, they can become sick. But God designed vultures with the ability to safely eat what could harm other creatures, and in so doing, they clean up creation.

The acid in a vulture's stomach is around one hundred times stronger than our stomach acid. It is even more potent than battery acid, and it successfully kills harmful bacteria. Through this special design, a vulture can safely eat decaying meat and get the nutrients it needs, and nature has an excellent crew to take care of the dangerous, unsightly problem of dead animals.

Staying Clean

If you have ever eaten meat from a bone, such as ribs or chicken wings, you know it's a messy meal! Now, imagine a vulture picking at dead meat. Did you picture the bird getting messy? Vultures not only help clean up dead animals but they also keep themselves clean while doing it.

If you look at a vulture, you might notice its bald face and neck. It does not have the most stylish haircut (or feathercut), but its appearance is very purposeful. Without feathers around their beaks, less food gets stuck on them as they eat. Vultures might have a messy job, but they care about their hygiene and keeping themselves clean. They can spend two to three hours a day preening, using their beaks like combs to tidy and straighten feathers. They also spread oil over their feathers from a gland (like a pocket) above their tails, which can help remove dirt and parasites. Vultures even take baths, submerging themselves in water to get more dirt off.

Time to Explore

Can you find a vulture or other scavenger bird eating an animal that has died? This can be hard to watch or even gross, but remember, they are doing the important work of cleaning up creation and keeping other creatures safe and healthy. Choose a way to help clean up God's creation today, like picking up trash from a park or natural area.

A Clean Heart

Have you ever heard anyone say that cleanliness is next to godliness? This is a familiar saying, but it is not from the Bible. This saying became popular after a theologian named John Wesley shared it in a sermon in 1791. However, God does have a lot to say about cleanliness, especially regarding our hearts.

We are all born into sin, and sin dirties up our hearts. It's not harmless dirt like we might get on our knees after an afternoon of playing outside. Instead, it's deadly dirt like the harmful bacteria that grows on roadkill.

Romans 3:23 says, "Everyone has sinned and fallen short of God's glorious standard." But there is wonderful news—Jesus came and died in our place, taking our deadly punishment for sin on himself so we can be clean before God. Second Corinthians 5:21 tells us Jesus had no sin, but he took our sin on himself: "Christ had no sin, but God made him become sin so that in Christ we could become right with God."

Because of Jesus's sacrifice, we can become right with God, and the dirt of sin can be removed from our hearts. All we have to do is tell God we are sorry for our sin (the wrong things we've done), accept Jesus's gift of salvation, and choose to follow Jesus with our lives. First John 1:9 says, "But if we confess our sins, he will forgive our sins, because we can trust God to do what is right. He will cleanse us from all the wrongs we have done."

Vultures have to work hard to keep themselves clean each day, but God has already done the heavy work for his children. He has made us clean through Jesus's sacrifice. While we live on a planet broken by sin's curse, we will still struggle with sin. But God helps us every day to live in ways that are free from sin as we wait to be in eternity with him, where there will be no sin at all and everything will be made fresh, clean, and wonderful.

If you have never asked Jesus to be your savior and to make you clean from sin, today is a great day to do that. It's the best decision you can ever make.

Dear God, thank you for designing vultures to help keep creation clean and healthy. Thank you for giving us a clean heart through Jesus and for helping us live with clean words and actions. Amen.

20

Sunfish

A Perfect Father

A Marvelous Shimmer

Have you ever seen something glittering beneath the water's surface? Maybe you were at a lake or a pond and a flash of shimmering color shot through the water or moved slowly next to the shore. It's possible you saw a sunfish. Maybe you've even caught one of these glimmering freshwater fish on a fishing line or with your hands.

There are around thirty-five different types of sunfish. What's often surprising is that smallmouth and largemouth bass are sunfish. Bluegill, a common freshwater fish often caught by fishers and admired for its blueish color, is also a species of sunfish.

All these fish belong to an order called ***Centrarchiformes***. Fish in this category have flattish bodies with spiky, raylike fins that you can feel pressing against your skin if you hold one. Sunfish show their marvelous colors when the sun reflects off their mosaiclike bodies, revealing a splash of color from God's studio of underwater lakes, ponds, and rivers. But how does God splash so many types of sunfish in a kaleidoscope of colors?

Color and Shine

The brilliant colors on a sunfish are not flat, like a printer might print red or blue ink on a piece of paper. They are crystal-like, which causes light to reflect and shine off them. God designed a sunfish with a mixture of color and shine, a bit like if you were to mix sparkles into paint. The color in a fish's skin is from special cells called ***chromatophores***. Chromatophore cells are like little packets of pigments, or colors. There are different types of these pigment cells, including red, black, orange, yellow, and brown.

The sparkle or shine on a sunfish is created by a different kind of cell called ***iridophores***. Iridophore cells have tiny crystal structures that act like mirrors, reflecting light and creating shimmering silver, blue, and green colors.

Sunfish can use these specially designed cells to change color in a way that's similar (but not as dramatic) as octopuses in the ocean. They can expand and contract the cells, like opening and closing them, to reveal or hide different colors. Male sunfish use this design when they brighten their colors to attract a mate during breeding season.

A Father Sunfish

While we're on the topic of mating season, sunfish have a unique way of raising their young. When it's time to mate, the male sunfish makes a nest underwater near the shore. He excavates an area using his fins and even his mouth to move rocks and create a smooth, saucerlike nest around twice the size of his body. He will use his flashy colors and a special dance to impress a female. If he succeeds, she will lay her eggs in the nest he made, and then her job is done, and she swims off. The male stays at the nest, carefully tending to the eggs. He guards them from predators and uses his fins to fan the eggs, moving water over them to keep them clean and provide fresh water with lots of oxygen so the eggs can develop into babies, called ***fry***. Once the fry hatch from their eggs, they will stay near the nest for several days. The father sunfish stays with them until they swim off on their own.

Time to Explore

Explore the shore of a lake, pond, or stream with your parent or an adult. Walk slowly so you do not scare fish away. Watch the water's surface for shadows or movement. Do you see a sunfish? Look for a flat-bodied fish with spiky fins and glistening colors. Write down each color you see in a notebook. Or use colored pencils to draw a sunfish and try to match its colors.

A Perfect Father

We can trust God to protect and provide for us because he is our perfect heavenly Father. Psalm 91:4 uses the image of a bird to teach how God carefully protects his children: "He will cover you with his feathers, and under his wings you can hide. His truth will be your shield and protection." This is a picture example, of course, so when we see a parent bird sheltering its eggs or chicks, we can remember how God gives us what we need and keeps us safe. However, birds are not the only creatures that make nests for their young. Other creatures that build nests to protect their babies include rabbits, squirrels, ants, foxes, and as we just learned, sunfish (along with many others)!

We can trust our perfect heavenly Father to protect us and provide everything we need. He never makes a mistake. He is all-powerful and knows everything. First John 3:1 says, "See what great love the Father has lavished on us, that we should be called children of God!" (NIV).

As a perfect Father, God shows us the way to go, patiently teaches and corrects us, and cares for us with a love that cannot be measured.

Unlike a young sunfish fry, which ventures off on its own and might never cross currents with its parents again, God guides, protects, and provides for us for our entire lives and into eternity.

Dear God, thank you for splashing the water with color and shine when you created sunfish, and thanks for making sunfish dads with the built-in knowledge of how to protect their babies. Thank you for being our heavenly Father and always knowing what we need. Amen.

21

Fox

A Wild Reputation

The Power of Play

Have you ever watched puppies playing together? They are very cute. I had the opportunity to watch wild puppies—fox babies (called ***kits***)—in my own neighborhood! Did you know foxes are wild dogs? They belong to the ***Canidae*** family, which includes domestic or pet dogs and wild dogs, such as foxes, wolves, and coyotes.

My family and I were driving home when we noticed a couple of small foxes on top of some dirt mounds. We pulled over and watched as the fox kits retreated to the safety of their underground den. The next day, when we drove by, we noticed a few more fox kits, bringing the total to six. We stopped again on the following day, and the entire family had come out to play. We counted twelve kits!

While most mother foxes give birth to around four or six kits in a litter, they can have up to twelve. We watched with big smiles and lots of laughter as the young foxes leaped on top of each other, pulled at each other's tails, and tumbled as they played chase. It was hilarious watching them play, and yet it's not all fun and games. Fox kits' play is important. As they chase, creep, huddle down, and leap, they are practicing important hunting skills they'll soon need to use. Their parents encourage them to play and will sometimes steal balls and other toys from neighborhood yards to bring back for their kits to play and practice with.

Just as a fox kit's play is important, so is yours! As you play outside, perhaps climbing trees, balancing across logs, or hiking on a trail, your body, brain, and spirit grow stronger. God designed foxes and people to enjoy playing and become stronger through it.

A Tricky Reputation

As the fox kits in our neighborhood grew older, their parents began taking them on field trips away from the den to learn how to hunt. Eventually, they stopped returning to the den. Over the summer, we would often see the kits, now much larger, roaming around our neighborhood and hunting for food.

Foxes' hunting habits have earned them a ***reputation*** for being sneaky troublemakers. Do you know what a reputation is? A reputation is what people tend to think about you, normally because of the way you act. Someone can have a good reputation for being funny, kind, helpful, smart, or creative. Someone can also have a bad reputation for lying or bullying.

Foxes have a reputation for being pests that hunt farmers' chickens and steal eggs from chicken coops. While we loved watching the foxes in our neighborhood, our neighbors who raise chickens were not excited about the new fox family and had to keep a close eye on their coops.

Even though foxes sometimes get a bad reputation for stealing a chicken or an egg, they can actually be very helpful to farmers and homeowners. Foxes eat a large number of small rodents, such as mice and voles, which destroy crops and often enter houses. This makes foxes a ***biological control***—a living creature that helps keep another creature's population from getting too big. Instead of using harmful chemicals or painful traps, God gave us natural helpers, like foxes, to maintain balance. Foxes remind us that God designed creation with built-in ways to stay healthy, even in a world that isn't perfect.

Time to Explore

Go outside with a parent or caregiver to look for a fox. Foxes are ***crepuscular***, which means they are mostly active at dawn and dusk. Find a quiet spot near a field, forest edge, or park and then sit still, listening and watching carefully. Even if you don't see a fox, write or draw what you noticed about the sounds, smells, and other animals you saw at that time of day.

A Wild Reputation

Do you think foxes try to have a reputation for being sneaky troublemakers? No, of course not. Foxes are not trying to be mean to farmers or chicken owners. Instead, they are trying to find food for themselves and often their families. Foxes hunt so they can live and have more foxes. They are helping their families and at the same time helping to keep nature in balance.

Foxes are not thinking about their reputations as they hunt, but we should consider our reputations. God's Word says we should be known as people who love and follow God and that the ways we live and behave can point others to God's truth and love. Matthew 5:16 says, "You should be a light for other people. Live so that they will see the good things you do and will praise your Father in heaven."

What are some things you can do so that others around you can see God's light? Consider the words you say (and the words you choose not to say) and how you show kindness to others. First Peter 2:12 says, "People who do not believe are living all around you and might say that you are doing wrong. Live such good lives that they will see the good things you do and will give glory to God on the day when Christ comes again."

As you study God's Word, follow his ways, and allow his Spirit to work in and through you, others will notice you are different, and that's good! We should have a reputation for living in God's ways and loving as he does.

Dear God, thank you for making foxes and other creatures that help keep nature in balance. When we see a fox, help us remember that we should have a good reputation for loving and helping others. Amen.

22

Snapping Turtle

Expert Fishers

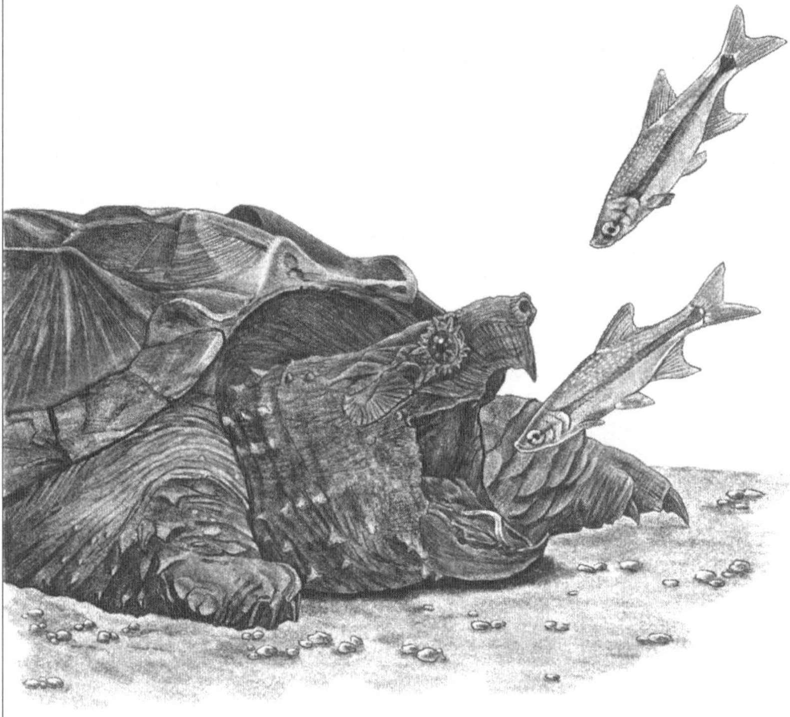

Don't Blink

What do you think of or feel when you think of snapping turtles? If you live near freshwater lakes, rivers, ponds, or marshes in North America, places where snapping turtles call home, these creatures might be something you fear.

I grew up exploring ponds near my family's home, and we were always on the lookout for snapping turtles. It's wise to be aware when snapping turtles might be nearby so you can give them space. Their snappy bite can cause a lot of harm. The alligator snapping turtle (located in the southern United States) is strong enough to break bones with its bite, which is where it gets its fierce name.

While turtles are normally known for being slow, snapping turtles do one thing incredibly fast: bite. Common snapping turtles can lunge forward with their snapping bite at 174 miles per hour, which is far faster than you can blink your eye, giving you a good reason to keep away from a snapping turtle's mouth!

Taking the Bait

While common snapping turtles stay fairly small (around the size of a dinner plate), the alligator snapping turtle can grow to be around two to two-and-a-half feet long. Males can weigh over two hundred pounds—as much as some adult humans. That is a large turtle! In fact, it's the largest freshwater turtle in North America.

The alligator snapping turtle's bite is slightly slower than a common snapping turtle's, but this is not a problem because God gave the alligator snapping turtle a unique way of tricking its prey. God equipped it with a built-in fishing lure.

An alligator snapping turtle's tongue has a special part that looks like a wriggling worm. This unique and smartly designed part of its tongue is called a ***vermiform lure***. The word *vermiform* comes from the Latin word meaning "worm-shaped."

Alligator snapping turtles are ***ambush predators***, which means they stay very still while they wait for prey to come near and then they attack quickly with their super-fast snapping bite. The turtle sets a fishing trap to catch its prey. It chooses a location and stays very still with its mouth wide open. The special wormlike part of its tongue sways back and forth in the water, looking just like a tasty worm. Hungry fish swim closer to inspect this possible snack, and if it's convincing enough, they get closer to gobble it up. But before they can get the "worm," the turtle attached to it snaps up the fish.

Why All the Snapping?

Why would God create animals like the alligator snapping turtle with its scary, fast, and powerful bite? God originally designed animals and humans to eat plants. That's why there are so many delicious and nutritious plants throughout the world. Genesis 1:30 says, "I have given all the green plants as food for every wild animal, every bird of the air, and every small crawling animal." After the worldwide flood, God added to the menu. In Genesis 9:3 he said animals could now be food: "Everything that moves, everything that is alive, is yours for food. Earlier I gave you the green plants, but now I give you everything for food."

God knows everything in humanity's past, present, and future. He gives creatures what they need to survive in a broken world so they can catch other animals for food. In God's care and thoughtfulness, he equipped snapping turtles with their quick bite and provided alligator snapping turtles with a built-in fishing lure to help them live and thrive.

Time to Explore

While it's not wise to get close to a snapping turtle, you can enjoy watching them from afar. Some zoos and nature centers have snapping turtles you can see up close. If you don't know where to find a snapping turtle, you can still enjoy observing other types of turtles at a pond, lake, aquarium, or zoo. Observe their slow yet intentional movements and their watchful eyes. What is one of your favorite things about how God designed turtles?

Expert Fishers

God designed alligator snapping turtles to be expert fishers. Humans have long fished to put food on their families' tables.

The New Testament shares many historical events related to fishing. Fishing was a way to feed one's family and was used for trade. Can you think of any stories in the Bible about fishing? How about:

- Simon's miraculous catch of fish (Luke 5:1–11)
- Jesus calling his first disciples to leave their livelihoods of fishing to follow him (Matt. 4:18–22)
- Jesus providing a coin inside a fish's mouth to pay taxes (Matt. 17:24–27)
- Jesus miraculously multiplying a boy's lunch of two fish to feed a massive crowd (John 6:8–15)

Fishing was important in Bible times, and it remains important today to feed people and animals. But in one of the above stories, Jesus spoke of a very different type of fishing. When Jesus called his disciples in Matthew 4:19 (and also in Mark 1:17), he told them to leave their fishing nets and become "fishers of men" (ESV). They wouldn't actually be capturing people; instead, they would be gathering people for God's kingdom. They risked leaving what made them money—fishing—to draw people into God's light by his truth and goodness.

We, too, can be fishers of people. Unlike a snapping turtle tricking and trapping prey, our kind of fishing is led by love, attracting people to God by living in his ways and spreading his gospel.

Dear God, thank you for creating alligator snapping turtles with a special lure so they can eat and stay alive. You thought of everything they would need! Help us to be fishers of people by drawing others to your great love. Amen.

23

Tree Bark

Layers of Protection

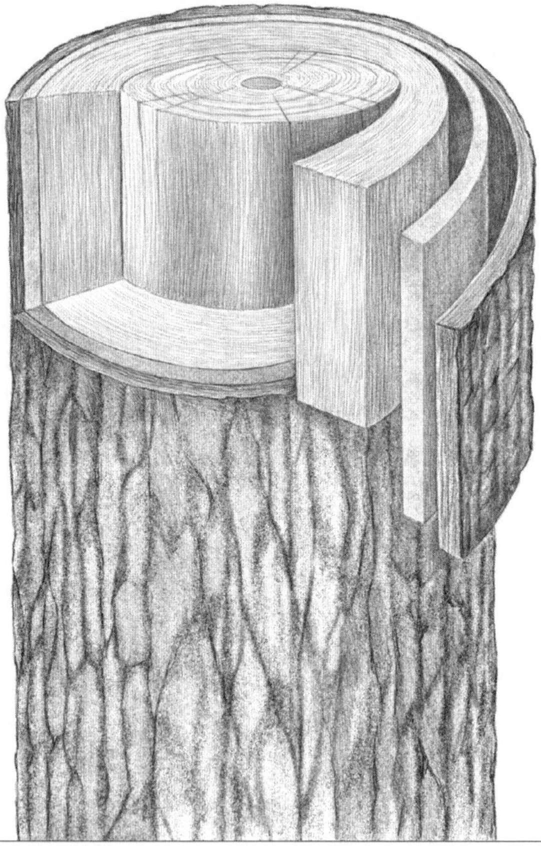

Tree Trunk Layers

Have you ever looked at tree bark? Perhaps you've noticed a tree with a thick, bumpy outer layer, like little mountain ridges. Bark doesn't only look cool; it also has the critical job of protecting a tree's trunk.

The trunk of a tree is strong and sturdy, and it helps the tree grow tall without toppling over. However, the trunk is not just a support structure; it also delivers water and nutrients up from the tree's roots and into its branches and leaves.

When we look at a tree trunk, we see the thick ***outer bark***. But a tree trunk is a bit like an onion with many layers. Under the thick outer bark is a layer of ***inner bark***, which helps transport nutrients to different parts of the tree. These nutrients also help create new wood. It is like a wood-making factory, adding new wood inside the tree trunk so the tree can grow wider. Just like all living things, as the tree grows, some of its older cells die, but those are not wasted; they become the protective outer bark as well as the ***heartwood*** inside the tree.

Bark Designs

When you think of tree bark, what do you picture? Maybe you think of trees in your yard or neighborhood. Do they have thick, bumpy bark, or is it smooth? Is it dark brown, red, or white? God designed many types of trees. Some trees grow fruit to snack on. Other trees produce nuts that we can add to cookies or trail mix. Different trees create different types of wood that humans use in making buildings, furniture, paper, and other products. God displays his creativity and care through many different kinds of trees. Can you think of anything you used today that came from a tree?

Just as humans design clothes to serve different purposes—fancy outfits for special occasions, winter coats to keep warm, and raincoats to stay dry—God designed tree bark to be both beautiful and useful. Outer bark not only protects the important inner bark layer but it also protects a tree from insects that want to burrow into its wood. In addition, bark protects and insulates a tree from extreme weather and fire. Bark holds essential water inside a tree and keeps harmful fungus and bacteria out.

Bark Homes

Bark isn't only helpful for protecting trees. It also provides habitats and helps other living things. Beautiful lichens (part fungus and part algae) as well as moss grow on tree bark, making many trees look like they are painted bright green and orange.

Insects and some amphibians crawl beneath loose tree bark to stay safe. Some insects even wait out the cold winter months in cozy homes beneath tree bark. When bark peels off and falls from the tree to the forest floor, that bark is eaten by tiny living organisms that turn it into healthy soil so new trees and other plants can grow.

Many animals, including beavers, squirrels, and deer, eat the inner bark of trees, which is full of nutrients. Beavers chew through the tough outer bark to get to the rich inner bark. This is especially important in the winter months when other food is hard to find. Did you know that humans eat bark too? Cinnamon sticks are the dried inner bark of cinnamon trees. If you have ever enjoyed cinnamon in cookies or ice cream, you've snacked on inner tree bark!

God designed trees to be able to heal and repair themselves, like how your skin grows a new layer after you scrape your knee. If a deer nibbles on tree bark, the tree can grow new bark in place of what was eaten. However, if too much bark is eaten, it can cause harm to the tree. Tree bark is a reminder of how God designed beautiful balance in nature.

When God fashioned trees, he carefully considered how to protect them with bark and devised creative ways to utilize it to help other living things.

Time to Explore

Go outside and look for different types of tree bark. Don't peel the bark off a tree—it needs it for protection. But feel the texture. Study its rough ridges or smooth surface. Sketch the bark in a notebook and see if you can match its colors and patterns. If you find bark on the ground, collect it and try to identify the tree it came from.

Layers of Protection

When we look at a tree, we can admire the beautiful bark on the outside, but we do not see the important inner bark layer beneath. The hidden inner bark layer is what keeps the tree strong and growing year after year.

The Bible says we have something like that inside us too. Ephesians 3:16 says, "I pray that out of his glorious riches he may strengthen you with power through his Spirit in your inner being" (NIV). What do you think your inner being is?

Our inner being is our spirit, the part of us that God made to live forever. We aren't only made of skin, bones, and blood. God made us in his image, with an everlasting spirit that he strengthens and grows from the inside out.

Just as the inner bark layer helps a tree grow and the outer bark protects it, God's Spirit inside us helps us grow stronger in faith and protects our hearts. We don't create our own strength—God does that in us!

Trees can live for many years, but one day they stop growing. Their bark falls away, and the tree returns to the soil. But because God gave us an everlasting soul, even as our bodies grow older, God's Spirit stays inside us, making us strong.

Second Corinthians 4:16 says, "So we do not give up. Our physical body is becoming older and weaker, but our spirit inside us is made new every day."

When we trust God to care for our hearts like the outer bark protects the inner bark, we can keep growing in faith no matter what comes our way.

Dear God, thank you for wisely making trees with bark to protect themselves and to help nature. Likewise, thank you for keeping our inner person safe and strong. Please keep growing our faith and protecting our spirits. Amen.

24

Monarch Chrysalis

Searching for Gold

A Caterpillar's Cozy Place

Think back to a time when you tried something new that you didn't know how to do. Maybe it was the first time you rode a bike or swam. Was it scary?

God designed caterpillars to do something they have never done before: to create a ***chrysalis***! A chrysalis is not something a caterpillar finds, like a hermit crab finding and choosing a shell to stay safe inside. Instead, the caterpillar makes a chrysalis using material from its body. The chrysalis is actually part of the caterpillar's body, called an exoskeleton, like an outer shell. God designed a caterpillar to sense when it is time to create its chrysalis. The caterpillar goes through its final ***molt***, shedding its outer caterpillar shell. At the same time, it creates its chrysalis, or new outer shell, which it will rest inside as it grows into a butterfly.

A Changing Chrysalis

Do you ever work on a piece of art over a few days, or even a week? Great art can take time, and the same is true for a monarch chrysalis. The creature stays inside the chrysalis for around eight to fifteen days. If you watch closely, you can see the chrysalis changing each day.

I once raised a monarch caterpillar and took a picture of its chrysalis each day until it hatched, noting how it looked a little bit different each day. Right after the caterpillar creates its chrysalis, it seems soft, squishy (but don't touch it!), and light green with yellow stripes. The following day, it looks very different. The shape is more rigid and defined, with a black, gold-studded band like a tiny tiara on top. The color is more lime green throughout, and it has lost its yellow stripes. There are magnificent golden studs near the bottom of the chrysalis, as if God used a paintbrush to carefully place finishing touches on the chrysalis. However, the creativity is not yet done!

Over the following week or so, the golden rim and studs become even more dazzling, and the chrysalis turns to a darker jade green. It is wonderful to watch the chrysalis through the entire process but especially the couple of days before the new butterfly emerges. The chrysalis appears to darken significantly at the bottom, but this is not a new color. Instead, it is losing color and turning see-through. The darker color you begin to see is the butterfly's dark wings! The day the butterfly emerges, the chrysalis turns completely see-through, revealing the beautiful black, white, and orange patterns on its wings. Although the chrysalis itself is see-through, the golden rim and studs remain, adorning the butterfly inside with beautiful jewels.

Once the butterfly emerges (called ***eclosing***), the creature is done with its golden jewels. They disappear, and the chrysalis is a thin, fragile, see-through shell.

Why the Dazzling Gold?

Scientists have theories, but they are not exactly sure why the monarch chrysalis develops a golden ring and studs. Some think it may cause birds to think twice before snagging a toxic monarch chrysalis for lunch, or it might help the developing butterfly inside get oxygen to breathe.

God designs things in nature with great purpose. If the golden studs keep the magnificent creature inside safe, they are evidence of God's careful care for the insect. If the golden studs are simply there to be beautiful, they show God's attention to detail and love for beauty. The closer we look at nature, the more splendor we see in every tiny detail.

Time to Explore

Look for a monarch chrysalis hanging from milkweed plants by kneeling or lying on the ground to see beneath the leaves. You can also gently turn over leaves to look for tiny eggs. If it's not the right time of year or you don't live in a place where monarchs are found, look for something else with beautiful colors that shine, such as a glimmering beetle, a bird's feathers shimmering in the sun, a rainbow, or sparkling snow. Perhaps write a poem about a caterpillar growing into a butterfly in its chrysalis.

Searching for Gold

A monarch's chrysalis isn't made of real gold. Its shine comes from natural materials God designed, including a color pigment called ***carotenoid***. The raised, 3D studs also reflect light, which makes the chrysalis look golden.

Although the golden studs are not made of actual gold, they are incredibly valuable because God calls them good. When God spoke everything in nature into place, he said it was all good. What God calls good, we should also call good and seek to protect it and share it with others.

People around us might want to convince us that certain things are good, but are they? We should not believe everyone when they say something is good. What matters is if God calls it good.

We can know what is truly good and valuable by reading and memorizing God's Word, the Bible, which is worth far more than genuine gold, and by asking God through prayer to show us what matters to him. Psalm 119:72 says, "Your teachings are worth more to me than thousands of pieces of gold and silver."

What is one way you can search for God's truth, which is more valuable than anything on earth? Decide today how you want to gather up the gold of his wisdom and love. And the next time you see a monarch, think of the gold decorations on its chrysalis, and remember God's Word is worth far more than actual gold!

Dear God, thank you for creating beautiful things in nature, including the monarch's chrysalis. Thank you for your Word and your Spirit, which reveal to us what is truly good and valuable. Help us to search for what is worthy and beautiful in your sight. Amen.

25
Wild Grass

God Doesn't Change

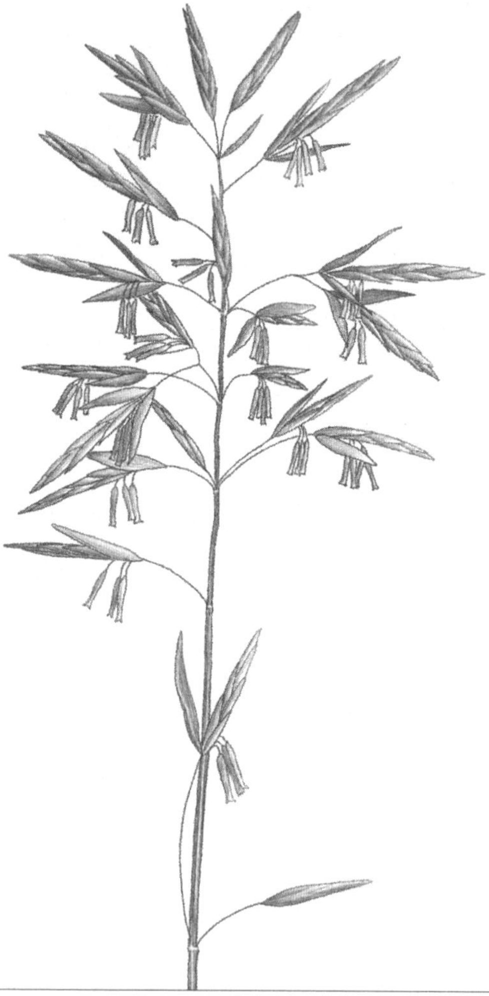

Grass Is Not Simple

Have you ever given much thought to grass? Maybe you enjoy sitting on or walking barefoot through grass in the summer, when it's soft. You might think of grass as a simple green plant, but it is not simple at all. Did you know God designed over twelve thousand different types of grass? His creativity goes far beyond the "simple" grass in many people's yards.

This beautiful planet is blanketed in many wild grasses. Grass grows on every continent, and even in harsh areas like the tundra ecosystem. When my family goes on summer hikes in the Rocky Mountains at over twelve thousand feet in elevation, we find grass! We can see God's artistic style in grasses as the different species follow a pattern. All plants in the ***Poaceae*** family have hollow stems. They have long, slender leaves, and their roots spread wide and are intertwined, which helps hold soil together.

Grass provides hay for animals to eat. Rice, wheat, oats, barley, and sugarcane also come from grass. If you eat bread or pasta, you have eaten something made from grass! Every type of grass also produces flowers.

Flowers from Grass

The flowers that grasses make are different from wildflowers blooming in a field or a bouquet of flowers you might buy at a store. Grass flowers do not have beautiful petals like most flowers; they are small and often go unnoticed. Grass flowers can be found inside a small part of the plant called a ***spikelet***. A spikelet is like a wrapped package that holds all the parts of the grass's flowers.

One day in June I was walking next to a field in our neighborhood. I noticed something hanging from the wild grass. It looked like tiny yellow bells were dangling from the end of the grass stems. What I saw are called ***anthers***. The anthers are a part of the flower that holds pollen, and they are very important for the grass, as they help it make seeds so more grass can grow across God's wild and wonderful world.

Surprising Grass

You might be surprised to find that some plants you already know are part of the grass family. If you enjoy corn on the cob or popcorn, you'll appreciate the fact that they're both made from grass! Corn is in the grass family, and so is bamboo. Do you remember how many types of grass God designed in the world? Over twelve thousand—and at least fifteen hundred of those varieties are different types of bamboo. The tallest growing bamboo, nicknamed giant bamboo or dragon bamboo, can grow up to one hundred feet tall, or around thirty meters (even taller in some cases). That's as tall as a ten-story building! Can you picture grass growing that high? God displays his incredible creativity in grasses around the world.

Time to Explore

Enjoy a nature walk and see how many different types of grass you can find. If you want to identify them, find a local grass identification guidebook or use a free app like iNaturalist. Or you can simply enjoy the different grasses by writing about their details or drawing them in a sketchpad. Break open a stem to see its hollow center and, depending on the season, see if you can find any parts of the grass flower.

God Doesn't Change

Have you ever stretched your arm out to feel wild grass on your fingertips as you walk through a field or natural area? My husband encouraged me to do this years ago, and now I often practice it while hiking and exploring. Different grasses can feel very different on your fingertips. Some are smooth, some are rough, some have ***seedheads*** at the tips. Grass also feels different depending on the season. It might feel smooth in spring when it is growing and full of water. In midsummer, it might leave dusty pollen on your fingertips. In late summer, as it turns brown or yellow and dries out, it might feel rougher. In winter, it might look dead. However, as it is a ***perennial*** plant that grows back each spring, it is only resting.

Wild grass changes how it looks and feels depending on what time of year it is. However, even grass that grows back each spring will eventually die. Isaiah 40:8 reminds us of this: "The grass dies and the flowers fall, but the word of our God will live forever."

Grass, like everything else in nature, is temporary. It will not last forever, but the God who created it will! And as this verse in Isaiah reminds us,

God's Word is also eternal. It does not wither or fade like grass dropping its flowers. Psalm 102:25–26 says:

> In the beginning you made the earth,
> and your hands made the skies.
> They will be destroyed, but you will remain.

Whenever you see grass in your yard or at a park, remember God's detailed designs. Although his creations fade with time, he never does. We can depend on his truth and love forever. As Hebrews 13:8 assures us, "Jesus Christ is the same yesterday, today, and forever."

Dear God, thank you for designing so many kinds of grass to look beautiful and make tasty foods. We are so grateful that you never change or fade. When things around us feel uncertain, or we are afraid of big changes, help us to remember that you stay the same and we can always lean on your love and truth. Amen.

26

Wasp

Trading Fear for Understanding

What Good Is a Wasp?

I don't know anyone who is fond of wasps. In fact, many people fear them because of their painful sting. We can admire bees for making honey, but most wasps don't make honey, so people often wonder, *Is there anything good about wasps?* When God designed all creatures, he said his creation was good, and we can see his good design and purpose in wasps.

Like many other insects, wasps are nature's gardeners. They visit flowers to drink tasty nectar, which gives them energy. When they travel from flower to flower, they spread dusty pollen, helping more plants grow.

Wasps also serve as pest control. They prey on insects that feed on crops and gardens, helping control pest populations to protect growing plants. Wasps are a healthier way to control pests than using harmful chemicals.

They are also an important food for many creatures, including birds, amphibians, reptiles, and some mammals. But do these predators get stung when they eat wasps?

What's the Sting For?

Creatures that eat wasps may sometimes get stung, but it's less common than we might think. Most wasps do not sting. And only a handful of wasp species have a sting strong enough to hurt humans. Even in the types that do sting, such as yellow jackets, hornets, and paper wasps, only the females have a stinger. Some people have dangerous allergic reactions to the venom that bees and wasps inject through their stinger and should be extra careful to avoid them. But why do wasps sting in the first place?

Wasps that sting do so to protect themselves and (in social species that live together) their colonies. God never intended for wasps to hurt humans. A stinger is both a defense against harm and a way to get food. Many solitary wasps that live alone use their stinger to paralyze prey so it cannot move and they can eat it. Even a wasp's stinger has a purpose.

Paper Homes

Yellow jackets, hornets, and paper wasps construct special lightweight homes out of paper. Of course, they don't go to the store to buy paper; they make it! Wasps scrape wood fibers off trees or fences, mix them with their saliva (spit), and create a papery pulp to build their home. If you have ever made something out of paper-mache—a gooey substance made by mixing paper with water and glue—it's a bit like that.

Wasps that create homes with paper carry it back to their colony in their mouths, then they spread and shape it into the outer walls of the nest and tiny hexagon cells where their babies will hatch.

Have you ever wondered why wasps and bees build cells with six sides? Hexagons are a perfect shape for fitting the most storage cells and supporting the hive's structure. Other shapes would leave wasted space and not be as supportive. Wasp eggs will hatch into babies (called larvae) inside the cells. Adults then care for the babies by bringing them food. When the wasp larva is ready to become an adult wasp, it creates a cap over the cell by weaving silk from a gland (like a pocket) beneath its mouth. Inside, it grows into an adult wasp, then it chews its way through the silk cap and emerges from the cell.

God designed bees and wasps to know how to build their homes to support, protect, and grow the colony.

Time to Explore

See if you can convince a wasp to visit by placing a saucer of water mixed with honey, or a fresh piece of fruit like watermelon, on a table outside. Keep a safe distance away from the wasp in case it's a stinging variety. (If you have an allergy to wasps, watch from inside through a window.) Count the wasp's legs. Do you notice any stripes or other patterns on its body? Record your observations by writing them down or drawing what you see in a sketchbook.

Trading Fear for Understanding

It's good to respect creatures that have a way of harming us, such as a female stinging wasp. However, sometimes we fall prey to fear because we do not understand something God has made. That fear can keep us from appreciating God's amazing designs. God is a purposeful creator. Sometimes in this broken world, it's harder to see his reasons for making things, but as we look closely and learn why God made things, we can marvel at his plans.

When we see past a wasp's stinger, we can see God's goodness in the wasp's design and how useful it is in nature. Wasps are important gardeners, and they act as pest control. People can learn a lot from how wasps build smart, strong structures using simple materials.

Second Timothy 1:7 says, "God did not give us a spirit that makes us afraid but a spirit of power and love and self-control." We can trade fears of the unknown for knowledge and wisdom, understanding God's detailed designs in creatures and how to stay safe around them. As we protect ourselves from wasps by learning to identify different types and giving them space, we can also care for them as part of God's special creation.

A lot of good can happen as we grow in knowledge. Where can we get knowledge? Proverbs 2:6 says, "For the LORD grants wisdom! From his mouth come knowledge and understanding" (NLT). God gives us knowledge in his Word and also through his created world (Rom. 1:20).

The more we learn about God's wild and wonderful world, the more we can lay aside fear so we can marvel at his designs.

Dear God, thank you for making wasps to protect creation through gardening and pest control. We love seeing your goodness in nature. When we are afraid of a creature, help us to learn more about it, including how to stay safe and the amazing ways you designed it. Amen.

27
Sunflower

Face the Light

A Growing Sunflower

Have you ever noticed sunflowers turning to face the sun? Sunflowers are fun flowers that are easy to watch and identify because they are so large. It might seem strange to watch flowers, but if you pay close attention, you might see that they are busy all day long as they use the sun's energy to create their own food through a process called ***photosynthesis***. This process helps them grow just like eating healthy foods helps humans grow.

Sunflowers don't always turn to face the sun. They mainly do this when they are young because they have a lot of growing to do, much like a baby drinks lots of milk or a toddler eats throughout the day, as their bodies are growing fast. Just as a young person needs a lot of food for their body to grow, a young sunflower needs a lot of the sun's energy to make its own food so it can become bigger and stronger. To create all the food necessary for growth, a young sunflower will often face the sun and turn its large flower head throughout the day to follow the sun, allowing it to soak up as much energy as possible. But if flowers do not have brains and are unable to think, how does a young sunflower know to do this?

Plant Messages

A sunflower doesn't *think* like humans do. God designed humans with brilliant brains. With our brains, we can make decisions and think through things. A sunflower does not behave in the same way. Instead, all the tiny cells inside it react to different conditions to ensure the plant gets everything it needs. One way a plant does this is through the use of tiny chemical messengers called ***hormones***. We humans, along with animals, also have chemical hormones. God designed hormones as tiny messaging systems that help our bodies to do everything they need to do. Or in this case, to help a plant.

Different hormones deliver different kinds of messages throughout a plant. Some tell the plant when to grow more cells or to create more ***chlorophyll***, the green pigment that helps plants soak up the sun's energy. Other hormones signal the plant when to begin growing in spring and when to produce beautiful flowers. Some hormones deliver messages to a plant to stop growing in the fall when it needs to rest. Some hormones trigger fruit to ripen at just the right time, while others protect plants from animals munching on them by signaling to the plant to produce a bitter flavor the animal doesn't like. But what is the special hormone that makes a sunflower turn toward the sun to soak up energy?

Follow the Sun

Plants would never be able to grow without the sun, but because Earth rotates, the sun changes position in the sky throughout the day. To make sure his creation was cared for, God designed plants to follow and face the sun or turn toward it so they can receive the most sunlight at every hour. This process of growing in response to sunlight is called ***heliotropism***, and it causes plants to move and bend.

To grow toward the sun, God designed plants with a special hormone called ***auxin***. Auxin delivers a message to the plant that makes it grow longer cells on one side of its stem. Which side do you think these longer cells grow on, the shady side or the sunny side? They grow along the shady side of the stem. The longer cells on the shady side cause the plant to curve and bend in the opposite direction, toward the sun. This is what makes young sunflowers turn toward and follow the sun as it moves from east to west throughout the day.

As we learned above, only young sunflowers do this. Once they grow tall enough and their stems are sturdy, they don't need as much sunlight. Instead, they stay in place, usually facing east, to warm up in the morning so more pollinating insects will come visit and spread their pollen. Even without minds to think or make decisions, sunflowers and other plants were designed to react to the sun and get everything they need.

Time to Explore

Perform an auxin experiment in your home. You can do this with most leafy house plants. Place the plant near a bright window. Watch for a week or so as the plant bends toward the window to reach more sunlight. After a week, move the plant to the opposite side of the window and observe it for another week to see if it reverses its direction. The plant is constantly growing longer cells on the shady side, signaled by the auxin hormone, that causes the plant to bend toward the sun.

Face the Light

Can you imagine Earth without the sun? Nothing could live. Sunlight gives plants the energy they need, and plants are a significant source of food for animals and humans. Genesis 1:16 says, "So God made the two large lights. He made the brighter light to rule the day and made the smaller light to rule the night. He also made the stars."

When God spoke the sun into place, he put it in precisely the right spot to keep the earth warm and provide the energy plants need. The sun's design is no accident but a perfectly created system that allows for life on Earth.

The sun is an incredible source of energy and light. The Bible tells us that God himself is light! First John 1:5 says, "God is light, and in him there is no darkness at all."

Just as a young sunflower follows the sun throughout the day to get everything it needs, we should always turn to face and follow God's light. Unlike a mature sunflower that stops its sun-following activities, we never grow out of our need to follow God's light. We can always be growing in our faith, which requires a steady dose of God's light every day. What are some ways we can turn to follow and face God's light?

First, we can turn away from darkness or anything that goes against God's Word. That might be sinful habits, wrong attitudes, or watching, reading, or listening to anything that doesn't line up with Scripture.

Second, we can turn toward God's light by reading, studying, and memorizing his Word, worshiping him, spending time with others who love and follow God, and enjoying time in creation. Psalm 25:15 says, "My eyes are ever on the Lord" (NIV). Let us always chase after God's light in all our activities.

Dear God, we want to always follow your light. Help us to turn toward your light each morning and follow it throughout the day, like a young sunflower chasing the sunlight. Amen.

28

Squirrel

Common Chatter

Noticing the Ordinary

Squirrels are so common that we can easily walk right past them without paying attention. That is, until one of two things happens. We tend to notice squirrels when:

1. They perform skilled acrobatics, hanging upside down or making daring leaps, to rob our bird feeders of seed.
2. They make alarming, trilling calls from a nearby branch to let us know they are upset about how close we are, or to warn nearby squirrels of a possible threat.

I recently noticed a squirrel for a very different reason. My family and I were picnicking in the Rocky Mountains when a small pine squirrel ran past our picnic table. The squirrel made no sound. Instead, what caught my attention was the shape of its body, which seemed unusual. And it was! Because this squirrel was two squirrels. The larger one held another squirrel, only slightly smaller than itself, in its mouth. It was a mother carrying her baby to safety! I marveled as the baby squirrel curled its body around its mother's mouth as the mother ran up a tree trunk and into a nest.

Perhaps squirrels are worth our attention even when they are not raiding bird feeders or sounding alarms, for God has designed them in many wonderful ways and with important jobs in nature.

A Great Balancing Act

Do you have a favorite climbing tree? We have a tree house in our backyard, and my kids enjoy climbing up, sitting with a good book, listening to birds, and watching squirrels. And there are many squirrels to watch at that height, because squirrels are animals of the treetops.

God designed squirrels as master climbers. A squirrel hastily runs across tree branches, leaping through the air from one to the next, which might seem foolish, yet I've rarely seen a squirrel fall. How do they balance so well?

If you have tried to balance while walking across a log or a narrow ledge, what might you do to help your body stay upright? One strategy is to stretch your arms out at your sides, making it harder to tip over. The squirrel uses a similar strategy with its long, bushy tail. As a squirrel runs and jumps along tree branches, its tail acts as a counterbalance, helping it stay upright and on course.

God also equipped squirrels with strong legs and hips and sharp claws, which help them climb up, down, and across trees without falling. This great balancing act helps squirrels escape predators, find the food they need, and navigate quickly and safely.

Planting Forests

Sometimes a squirrel can be forgetful, which can be very helpful for a forest. While squirrels eat many different foods, they are fond of nuts and seeds. You can often spot a squirrel busy burying its food for a later meal. Have you ever hidden something only to later forget where you put it? A squirrel faces this problem too. When a squirrel buries a nut, such as an acorn from an oak tree, and then forgets about it, the acorn can sprout into a new baby tree. This is a common way new trees are planted. Without knowing it or meaning to, squirrels are important foresters, planting new trees for future generations of squirrels to climb and for us to enjoy.

Time to Explore

Collect a few acorns (or rocks if you can't find acorns) and bury them in the ground. Come back a week later and see if you can locate and dig them up. Do you think it's easy for squirrels to remember exactly where they hid their snack? As you try to locate your buried acorns, watch and listen for squirrels nearby. Can you see any balancing across tree branches? Do you hear any chattering above?

Common Chatter

Has a squirrel ever yelled at you? My family often practices walking quietly through the woods only to have our silence interrupted by a chatty squirrel. God designed squirrels with many essential ways of communicating, including barking, screaming, purring, and chattering. While these different ways to communicate are helpful to squirrels, they give them a reputation for being chatty.

God has created us with many ways to communicate, and we should be careful to use our words wisely. Proverbs 18:21 says, "The tongue can bring death or life; those who love to talk will reap the consequences" (NLT). Is it wrong to love talking? This depends on what we are using our words for. When we use our words only to draw attention to ourselves, it's not helpful. We can avoid useless chatter and appreciate the power of words as we use them to bless others. Ephesians 4:29 tells us how to do that: "When you talk, do not say harmful things, but say what people need—words that will help others become stronger. Then what you say will do good to those who listen to you."

What is one way you can use your words today to help others become stronger in faith? Let's be people known for using our words well and in ways that please God and benefit those around us.

Dear God, thank you for the power of words and for playful squirrels who remind us to avoid useless chatter. Help us to not be common chatterers but instead to use words to share your love and truth with those around us. Amen.

29
Sand

Countless Grains

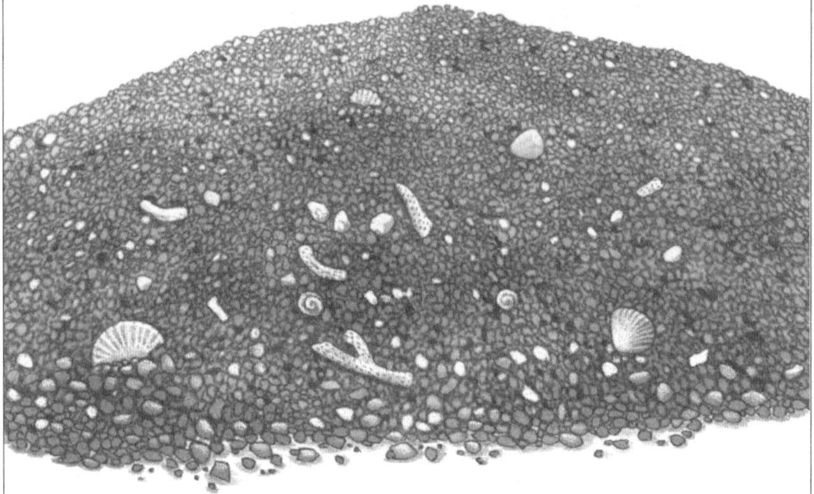

Sandy Structures

Do you enjoy building sandcastles? Sand behaves differently when wet or dry. If you try to build a sandcastle with dry sand, what happens? All the tiny grains probably slide right down and don't keep the shape you want. But if the sand you use is wet, the tiny sand grains stick together, allowing you to become a sand architect and build castles or other amazing structures. God designed sand to inspire us to create and be playful. But sand isn't only fun, it also helps many creatures.

Some animals, like crabs and clams, burrow into the sand to stay safe. Sand dollars even swallow sand—not because it's tasty, as you might know if you've ever accidentally had sand in your mouth—because it weighs them down. Swallowing sand helps young sand dollars anchor themselves to the ocean floor so they don't get swept away by strong currents. Some insects also make homes in the sand, including some types of bees and wasps. Caddisflies don't simply burrow in and make their homes. Instead, they create a safe, cozy home by wrapping themselves with sticky silk. Sand and other natural materials stick to the silk and create a protective tube-shaped house for the insect.

Animals also use sandy areas to nest. This includes turtles and shorebirds that lay their eggs in the sand. Seals and other marine mammals rest in sandy areas and raise their young there. Shorebirds also find food in sandy areas, picking insects or clams from deep in the sand with their long beaks. So, whether it's for building homes, raising babies, or snagging a meal, sand was created on purpose to support many of God's creatures.

Whenever you have the chance to create a sandcastle, remember all the creatures God created sand for! But what exactly is sand?

Tiny Grains

Have you ever held sand in your palm, then let it slip through your fingers? Did you look at the tiny grains before they slipped away? Some grains look the same but others are different. Sand comes from rocks and minerals. There are many types of rocks and minerals worldwide. Because of this, sand is unique since it can come from many different places. Each tiny sand grain was chipped from larger rocks or minerals through the process of ***erosion***. Erosion happens when rain, wind, or crashing waves break things down. Through erosion, rocks, minerals, shells, and coral skeletons get broken into tiny grains of sand.

If sand can be made from many different materials, what makes it sand? It is defined by its size. A sand grain measures from 0.0625 mm to 2 mm, but how tiny is that? It is around the same size as a sugar crystal. Sand is larger than dust but smaller than a tiny pebble. We can see individual sand grains with our eyes without having to use a microscope. If you laid sand grains side by side, it could take twelve or more to make a one-inch line.

Sand Art

Have you ever created sand art with brightly colored grains of sand from a craft store? That sand is colored in factories using dyes. But God dyed natural sand in many different colors too. Some sand is made from black volcanic rock, and other sand is chipped away from ***white quartz***. Quartz mixed with iron oxide makes yellow or brown sand. Rare pink sand is made from the shells of tiny living organisms called foraminifera. Bits of their red shells are broken down and mixed with grains of other shells and corals to make pink sand. God created amazing sand art around the world.

Time to Explore

Enjoy a morning or afternoon playing in the sand. With a parent or other adult, visit a sandy area near a lake, river, or ocean. Take a magnifying glass with you and look closely at the sand grains. What colors do you see? Can you tell if there are bits of shell in the sand or, if you're at the ocean, coral? Try to count the grains of sand. Can you see any animals using the sand as their home or to find food?

Countless Grains

Do you remember how sand is made? Waves, wind, and rain wear down rocks and other materials, turning them into tiny grains. This means new sand is always being created, especially by ocean waves.

In Psalm 139:17–18, the psalmist says God's thoughts are more than the grains of sand. Think about all the sand on Earth (it's impossible to imagine!) and consider how new sand is always being made. God has even more thoughts than that. What do you think he is thinking about? God thinks a whole lot about *you*, including how much he loves you and how he will take care of you!

Consider everything God created in the universe, from massive galaxies to tiny sand grains to even smaller living organisms that can only be seen through a microscope, and remember that he's thinking about *you* right now!

Psalm 139:1–3 says:

> Lord, you have examined me
>   and know all about me.
> You know when I sit down and when I get up.
>   You know my thoughts before I think them.
> You know where I go and where I lie down.
>   You know everything I do.

If you ever feel lonely or like no one understands what you are going through, remember the creator of the cosmos has more thoughts than there are grains of sand on earth, and you are always on his mind. He sees you, knows what you are going through, and has good, loving thoughts about you.

Dear God, thank you for making sand in so many colors and for designing it to help creatures live. Thank you for making it sticky when it's wet so we can build sandcastles. Thank you for thinking of us all the time. Help us to think about you more and more throughout our days. Amen.

30
Plant Gall

A Safe Shelter

An Insect Nursery

Have you ever walked through the woods and noticed a strange growth on a plant stem? Or maybe you have picked up a leaf that fell from a tree and noticed weird bumps on the underside. These growths and bumps found on plant stems and leaves are called galls, and they are insect nurseries!

In many cases, an insect such as a wasp or a mite will lay eggs on a plant that is actively growing, perhaps where it is developing a new stem. The mother insect chooses this spot carefully because she wants the plant to keep growing. In fact, she wants it to grow right around her eggs!

While laying eggs, the mother also produces an enzyme, which is a protein that speeds up chemical reactions in something that's alive. In simpler words, enzymes make things grow or happen quickly inside creatures, plants, and us. In this case, the mama insect uses an enzyme to make a plant grow quickly to surround her eggs. This new growth on the plant is called a gall and becomes a safe nursery in which her eggs can hatch.

Leaving the Nursery

I was hiking one day when I noticed a plant gall on a rose stem right above where new leaves were growing. The rose stem had spikes all over it, but the large, round gall was smooth. The gall looked like a balloon halfway up the rose stem, but it was not soft like a balloon. Instead, it was very hard. As I looked closely, I noticed small holes in the gall. What do you think those holes were from?

They were tunnels where insects had chewed their way out. An insect does not want to live inside a plant gall forever. Many species grow from their baby larva to adult form inside the gall before leaving the nursery. Some insects will spend a couple of years growing up inside a gall before chewing their way out.

Do Galls Harm Plants?

Plant galls might look alarming or like they should not be there. In some cases, if there are too many galls or if they are on a young plant, they can cause harm. Thankfully, most galls do not hurt plants. They might look a little bit unusual, which is why the rose plant gall caught my attention while I was hiking, but for the most part, the gall helps the insect's babies stay safe while not harming the plant.

Plant galls provide a safe place for baby insects to grow up, which helps creatures continue their God-given work of producing more of their own kind.

Time to Explore

When you are out exploring God's wild and wonderful world, search for growths on plant stems or small bumps on the undersides of leaves. Can you see any tiny holes where insects came out? Or might there still be insects growing up inside the gall?

Different insects create different kinds of galls. You can use an identification guide or an app like iNaturalist to help identify what insect created a gall.

A Safe Shelter

God designed gall-creating insects with a special way to keep their babies safe. The plant gall acts as a nursery and shelter. It can remind us of God's protection and that he is our shelter. Psalm 91:1–2 says, "Those who go to God Most High for safety will be protected by the Almighty. I will say to the Lord, 'You are my place of safety and protection. You are my God and I trust you.'"

While insects grow up and leave the safety of their galls, we can always return to God's shelter. In fact, God is always with us and he protects us wherever we go.

How has God protected you or someone you know in the past? Can you think of a specific story?

When I was fourteen, I was preparing to travel to Africa for two months. Before I left, I needed to visit a doctor for a checkup. During that doctor's visit, we discovered I have a rare health condition that needed to be treated with medicine. God protected me by making sure we knew I had this condition and could treat it while I traveled.

I can think of many ways God has been a shelter for my family and me. He protects our hearts, minds, and bodies. The next time you feel afraid or confused, remember that God is your safe shelter, and he is always with you. In the first verse of Psalm 91, we read that "those who go to God Most High for safety will be protected by the Almighty." How can we "go to God Most High"? Here are some ideas:

- Pray to God and tell him what you are worried about, then ask him to keep you safe and give you peace as you trust him as your shelter.
- Read other verses about God being your shelter, including Deuteronomy 31:8; Psalm 46:1; Psalm 121; and Nahum 1:7.
- Go for a nature walk (perhaps look for galls along the way) and remember that God provides for his creation and cares even more about those made in his image—humans like you and me.

Dear God, thank you for giving insect mothers a unique way to protect their babies. We find comfort knowing that you are our shelter and our safe place. Whenever we feel afraid or worried, help us to find peace and comfort by going to you in prayer. Amen.

31

American Robin

Worms for the Wise

A Familiar Friend

Have you ever seen a bird with an orange or red belly? American robins are one of the most familiar birds across North America and one of the easiest to learn to identify. Europe also has a robin called the European robin. Although both of these birds have *robin* in their names, they are two very different species. In fact, the American robin was named after the European robin. Early European settlers saw a bird with a red belly when they explored America, reminding them of the European robin, which has an orange belly. They called it robin after the bird they knew back home. Another way to identify an American robin is by the white ring around its eyes.

The American robin is in the ***thrush*** family, along with wood and hermit thrushes. God orchestrated an excellent choir when he designed birds in this family. They have a special voice box (called a ***syrinx***) that can make two different sounds, including a rising and falling note, simultaneously. This allows them to sing beautiful, complex songs.

The Early Bird Gets the Worm

Have you heard someone say "The early bird gets the worm"? This common saying suggests that waking up early can lead to getting a lot done or securing the best opportunities. Robins are known as early birds. They are the first birds I hear singing in the morning, before the sun climbs over the horizon. I am an early riser, but the robins wake up before I do.

In the American robin's case, the early bird indeed gets the worm. Although American robins eat berries and many insects, worms make up a big part of their diet. They can eat up to fourteen feet of worms daily! Not all the worms robins pull from the dirt are for themselves; many are for their babies, called ***chicks***. The mom and dad robins feed their chicks, which hatch from light-blue eggs. Have you ever found a hatched robin's egg? They are a beautiful color.

American robin parents stay very busy feeding worms and insects to their chicks. They do this by first eating the food and then spitting it back up into their chicks' mouths. They feed their chicks this way for the first four days after hatching. The chicks ***fledge***, or fly away from the nest, after about thirteen days, but their parents' jobs are not done. The chicks continue to be fed by their parents for at least three weeks. You can sometimes see young birds, called ***fledglings***, lined up on tree branches with their parents feeding them.

Smart Timing

Other than early mornings, have you noticed another time when there are a lot of robins out searching for worms? Robins know that one of the best times to find worms is after a fresh rainfall. Rain causes worms to wriggle toward the surface of the soil. Although robins are not actually wise, they are intelligent and make the most of an opportunity to find the worms they need.

You can also often spot robins searching for worms in a lawn that has recently been mowed. Whether it's early morning or after a rainfall or lawn mowing, robins know how to make the best use of their time, finding worms when they're most likely to succeed in their search.

Time to Explore

If you have a lawn, consider conducting an experiment: Mow your grass, then turn on a sprinkler or hose. This should help bring worms to the surface. Once you've turned the water off, watch to see if robins come searching for them. Or go on a walk after it rains and see if you can spot robins looking for their next meal.

Or go on a walk in the morning, particularly after it rains, and look for robins searching for worms. Can you see one pulling a worm from the soil?

Worms for the Wise

You have a lot of choices to make every day. It can be hard to choose between sleeping in and getting up early for a morning walk. Or playing at a friend's house or going on a fun errand with a parent. As you grow older, you'll have more opportunities. Some will be to enjoy fun things and others will be to do meaningful work.

What do you think of when you hear "The early bird gets the worm"? A saying like this can either remind us to make the most of opportunities or make us afraid that we are missing out.

A robin can remind us that we don't need to be afraid of missing out, because we never miss out on the best things when we follow God's plan. Instead, we can make the most of every opportunity. Ephesians 5:15–16 says, "Look carefully then how you walk, not as unwise but as wise, making the best use of the time, because the days are evil" (ESV).

Can you think of ways to make the best use of your time? Here are some ideas:

- Wake up early to spend time with God.
- Pray and ask God for wisdom when you have a decision to make.
- Don't waste time, but instead use it to enjoy God's creation and learn more about him.
- When God gives you an opportunity to grow in faith or do good work, work at it with all your heart, mind, and strength as you trust him.

Just as robins wake early or head out after rain and don't miss an opportunity for good hunting, we can be wise in how we use our time, making the most of the opportunities God places in front of us.

Dear God, we don't want to miss out on the opportunities you bring our way. Help us to be like a robin, working hard to make the best use of our time. Amen.

32

Oak Tree

Designed for Strength

A Symbol of Strength

Picture a strong tree in your mind. If you envisioned something strong and tall, it might be an oak tree. Oak trees have long served as a symbol of strength. God designed oak trees to be tough and resilient and to live and grow for many years. An oak's wood is solid, making it very useful. Throughout history, oak wood has been used to make ships, barrels, homes, and furniture. Oak trees have wide trunks and thick branches. Perhaps you have enjoyed climbing the strong limbs of an oak tree before. Because they are so sturdy, oak trees can remain standing even when turbulent storms roll through.

The strength of oak trees is impressive. However, instead of only admiring the oak tree, we should always be reminded of a much greater strength—the power found only in our Creator God who designed the oak tree.

An Oak Tree's Beginning

Like most plants, an oak tree starts out as a seed. The seed of an oak tree is inside the oak tree's nut (a type of hard fruit), which is called an acorn. Perhaps you have found acorns before. They are smooth with a rough cap on top that can sometimes pop off. Acorns are fun to play with and are also very helpful for creatures.

Acorns help animals like deer, bear, squirrels, and chipmunks get the nutrition and calories they need, especially as they head into winter months. Psalm 147:9 (NLT) tells us that God "gives food to the wild animals," and Psalm 104:27–28 talks about how God opens his hand to feed the wild creatures. Acorns from oak trees provide much-needed food, allowing God's creatures to live and fill the earth with beauty and wonder.

So, an acorn can grow into a tall, strong oak tree, or it can make forest animals strong with healthy fats, carbohydrates, and vitamins. That's a strong tree!

An Oak Tree's Inner Strength

Have you ever heard someone talking about inner strength? Inner strength can refer to the strength within our spirit. Trees, of course, do not have the same kind of inner strength as humans because they do not have spirits. However, they have a different type of inner strength inside their microscopic ***cells***.

Every living thing on Earth is made up of tiny cells that we can typically only see while using a microscope. Each cell is like a small factory with many, many parts working together to help living things grow and stay alive. These tiny cell factories reveal God's wisdom as a great designer.

The cells in plants differ from those in animals and humans. Animals and humans have cells that are held together inside a flexible ***cell membrane***, like an elastic balloon. Plant cells, however, are much more rigid and unbending. Instead of a flexible membrane, plant cells have a ***cell wall***, which helps plants stand up and grow without having bones.

Have you noticed how a tree branch is much stronger than a flower stem? Both trees and flowers are plants made of plant cells, but woody plants, including trees, are extra strong.

Inside each tiny wood cell, God built an extra-thick wall called the ***secondary cell wall***. It's packed with strong fibers called ***cellulose*** and a natural glue called ***lignin***, which together make oak trunks—and other trees—tough and strong.

An oak tree's extra-thick cell walls are the reason it can sway without breaking during a windy storm and remain rigid and strong for hundreds of years.

Time to Explore

Go looking for acorns and make some acorn art. If you spot a lot of acorns in one place, look up! You might find an oak tree towering above. Use a fine-point permanent marker to draw faces on the acorns, using their caps as hats or beards or whatever else you can imagine. Use glue and tiny twigs, felt, or googly eyes to turn acorns into animals like owls, mice, or insects. Or leave acorns in a natural area as food for critters. Return later to see if perhaps a chipmunk left acorn crumbs and caps behind.

Designed for Strength

God designed oak trees to be strong and to give strength to animals through their acorns. In a similar way, God made us to be strong and to offer strength to others. Ephesians 6:10 says, "Be strong in the Lord and in his great power."

An oak tree does not make itself strong. Instead, it grows strong because God wrote special DNA into oak trees that tells them to grow extra-thick cell walls. Likewise, we don't muster our own strength through willpower or positive thoughts alone. Instead, we realize our God-given strength as we follow his plans.

As we live more and more by God's strength instead of our own, we can help others grow stronger in their faith. Romans 15:1–2 tells us, "We who are strong in faith should help the weak with their weaknesses, and not please only ourselves. Let each of us please our neighbors for their good, to help them be stronger in faith."

Why not look for ways to let God be your strength today? If you feel weak, ask him to show up with his power and to reveal opportunities to help others realize God's strength in their lives.

Dear God, thank you for making strong oak trees grow from small acorns. Your designs are smart and reveal your power. Help us to see your strength in our lives and to show others your power also. Amen.

33
Great Blue Heron

Claiming What's Yours

Birds with Mohawks

Have you ever seen a bird with a mohawk? Many birds have long feathers that stand up on their heads, resembling a mohawk hairdo. These fancy head feathers are called a ***crest***. One of the most impressive crests I have seen is on the great blue heron.

Male herons will raise their jet-black crest feathers to look larger and more impressive, to attract a mate, or to intimidate and warn off an intruder. These remarkable birds can stand around four feet tall on their long, stilt legs. They use their long necks to go spearfishing. You might spot a heron standing still as a statue so as not to be noticed, or wading very slowly and carefully through shallow waters while looking for fish beneath the water's surface.

I love approaching a heron, whether on my feet or on a paddleboard, and trying to move slower than even it does. Watching its impressive fishing act is great fun! Once a heron spots a fish, it rapidly shoots its long neck down, plunging its beak underwater to either spear or catch the fish, before promptly swallowing it. I've watched a heron do this with a sunfish larger than my hand, swallowing it whole right before my eyes.

A Bird Nursery

Every March, great blue herons return to our neighborhood. I know spring is near when I spot the first few as they perch on top of power line posts, trees, and neighbors' roofs. They return at the same time each year to claim what is theirs: an island in our lake. The island has many tall cottonwood trees holding up large birds' nests made from sticks. The herons return year after year to raise their young on our lake. Herons are ***colony birds***, which means they nest together and raise their young in large groups.

The island is called a ***rookery***. A rookery is an area where different types of birds gather to build nests, lay eggs, and raise their young. On our rookery, great blue herons claim the large nests in the treetops. We also usually have a few pairs of another kind of heron called a black-crowned night heron. Red-winged blackbirds nest in lower branches, and geese lay eggs in ground nests below the trees, near the water's edge.

By the middle of summer, the rookery is alive with movement and noise. I love paddling out to watch from a respectful distance as parent great blue herons return, swoop down, and land on their nest to feed their young with fish.

Taking Back What's Theirs

The trees on our rookery are prime real estate for birds, which means many birds want to nest there. The island is quiet and safe, as no large predators, such as foxes or coyotes, can get to the island to snatch eggs. God designed birds with instincts to search out safe places to raise their young, and the island is such a place.

Some weeks before the great blue herons return from their migration journeys, other birds try to snag the best nests. We've seen a bald eagle try to set up home on the island several weeks before the herons are due to return. One year, dozens of black cormorants showed up, lining the cottonwood tree branches and staking out the island. When the herons arrived, they had a difficult task of moving back in and convincing the cormorants to find another nesting place. Yet year after year, the herons succeed in claiming what is theirs.

Male herons return first to the rookery and use their mohawks, along with their impressive calls, to intimidate other birds away from the nesting site.

God designed male herons to have even more remarkable mohawks during breeding season. They grow long decorative ***nuptial plume*** feathers, which help them attract a female. These nuptial plume feathers also prove helpful in intimidating other birds away from the nesting site.

Male herons have the critical task of staking out the rookery as they wait for the females to arrive. Once the females join them, the herons work hard at preparing their nests. They will often fix up old nests or sometimes build new ones. I enjoy watching them over several weeks as they gather materials and ready the rookery for a new generation of great blue herons.

Time to Explore

Enjoy a nature walk near a lake, pond, river, or the ocean. As you walk, look for birds searching for food. Do you see any birds sticking their long beak beneath the sand to get insects? Can you find a heron carefully scanning the water in search of a fish? Stop and closely observe the bird gathering food. Use a local field guide or a free app like Merlin Bird ID to help identify and record the birds you see.

Claiming What's Yours

Have you ever had something taken from you, perhaps by a sibling or friend, and then you responded by saying something like, "Hey, that's mine!"? After a moment like this, you were probably encouraged by an adult to practice sharing. It's good to exercise our sharing muscles and allow others to enjoy things alongside us. However, in some cases, it's good to claim what is ours. I am not saying it's okay to fight over a toy that a friend picked up, but instead, we can lay claim to what God says belongs to us.

The enemy, Satan, wants to steal from us. John 10:10 says, "The thief comes only to steal and kill and destroy; I have come that they may have life, and have it to the full" (NIV).

Can you think of anything Satan might want to steal from you? He will try to steal God's peace from your heart and God's promises from your mind. But as we just heard, John 10:10 tells us Jesus came to give us life to the fullest—a life overflowing with his love, joy, and peace. We don't need to let the enemy take what is ours. Ephesians 3:19 says, "Christ's love is greater than anyone can ever know, but I pray that you will be able to know that love. Then you can be filled with the fullness of God."

When we hide God's Word in our hearts, memorize his promises to us, and feel his peace as we pray, the enemy can no longer steal from us. Like a heron claiming and protecting its nesting site from other birds that want to take it, we can claim what God says belongs to us and not allow the enemy to move in and take over.

Dear God, thank you for your promises that pile high in your Word, the Bible. You give us a life full of your love, truth, peace, and hope. Help us to hide your Word in our hearts so the enemy cannot steal what belongs to us. Amen.

34
Fireweed

Growing After Hard Times

A Bright Pink Carpet

Have you ever seen a forest after a wildfire comes through? It can be very sad to see the scorched, blackened trees. However, wildfires serve a natural purpose. As long as the fire is not a threat to human lives, we can see it in a positive light as it refreshes a forest. But how can fire be good?

Sometimes dead tree branches, pine needles, leaves, and other natural things pile up on the forest floor, like a bedroom with toys and clothes strewn about. If there are too many things piled up, the bedroom floor can no longer be seen. This clutter is harmful in a forest as it keeps new plants from growing. A healthy fire can burn away old forest debris and clear the way for new growth. Sometimes that new growth is a vibrant pink carpet of fireweed flowers.

Fire-Resistant Rhizomes

Fireweed has stems that grow underground, called ***rhizomes***, which are resistant to fire. While a fire might burn the plants above ground, the rhizome stems underneath are protected. Once the fire passes, the plant's rhizomes can work hard at producing new, fresh shoots, which then grow leaves, stems, and flowers that produce pollen and seeds so new fireweed plants can grow.

When hiking, someone might not even know there is fireweed where they are exploring. The plant is beneath the ground, waiting for the right conditions to sprout and grow above the soil.

Fireweed not only helps to make a burned area look beautiful again but it also provides much-needed food for wild creatures. Fireweed flowers provide sweet nectar for pollinating insects. Fireweed also helps stabilize the forest floor after a fire, reducing erosion so the soil can stay together and strong, and lessening the chance of flooding as it catches rainwater.

Designed to Spread

Fireweed grows very well and in abundance because of the way God designed it to spread. Each flower can produce a seed capsule with three hundred to five hundred seeds. It's estimated that a single fireweed plant can produce around eighty thousand seeds, each with the potential of spreading, germinating, and growing a new fireweed plant. But how do its seeds spread?

Fireweed does not have legs, of course. It cannot walk around the forest floor scattering its seeds on the soil. So instead, God designed it with a fun and whimsical way of spreading its seeds: on the wind! When a seed is carried to a new area by the wind, it's called ***wind dispersal***. Seeds that are spread through wind-dispersal are often light, and God engineered many, including fireweed seeds, with fluffy parachutes. A fireweed seed's parachute is made from silky strands that catch easily in the wind. When the wind blows, it carries the seeds away from the parent plant, sometimes far, far away. This helps the seeds land in new places to grow where they'll have space, sunlight, and soil.

When fireweed seeds spread across the burned forest floor, they grow well because the soil is rich in minerals from burned natural materials.

Fireweed is one of the first plants to grow in the aftermath of a wildfire, and it is specially designed to welcome life back to a meadow or forest.

Time to Explore

Have you ever seen a wind-dispersed seed in the air? Cottonwood trees are known for their cottony seed parachutes. Milkweed and dandelions are also designed with seed parachutes. Go outside on a breezy day and see if you can spot plant seeds, such as cotton from a cottonwood tree, riding on the wind. Or pick a dandelion seedhead and blow on it to watch the seed parachutes spread.

Growing After Hard Times

Wildfires can be very sad. My family has experienced several wildfires where we live in Colorado, including the largest wildfire in Colorado's written history and a smaller fire that burned so close to our home that we nearly had to evacuate. God values human lives more than the rest of his creation, because we are made in his image, so fires are not good when they threaten human lives. But in a forest away from humans, they can refresh the land and prepare for new growth.

Have you ever been through a wildfire? Maybe there wasn't an actual forest fire burning close to your home but a challenging circumstance in life. Sometimes God uses hard things in life to grow us. Think about wildfires, which can be very bad, yet in the right conditions, they can also prepare the way for new life.

Romans 5:3–5 says, "We also have joy with our troubles, because we know that these troubles produce patience. And patience produces character, and character produces hope. And this hope will never disappoint us, because God has poured out his love to fill our hearts. He gave us his love through the Holy Spirit, whom God has given to us."

God doesn't want us to have to go through hard things, but he can use difficult circumstances to grow our faith and bring new life to our spirit.

When you go through hard things, picture fireweed and ask God to grow your heart in beauty and strength.

Dear God, thank you for using even the hard things in life to grow our faith. Thank you for designing beautiful fireweed to carpet a forest in color and to bring new life after fire. Amen.

35
Chipmunk

Following Curiosity's Trail

Chipmunk or Squirrel?

Have you ever watched a small striped chipmunk curiously poke its head from behind a rock to see if you have any food to offer it? When my family and I explore the Rocky Mountains, we see many of these cute, curious creatures. Just this week, we were picnicking in the mountains and a small chipmunk kept running near, far, and everywhere in between our picnic area, searching for dropped crumbs.

The chipmunks we encounter are often comfortable with humans and seem to know that hikers always carry snacks. Although human snacks are not suitable for chipmunks, it is fun to watch these critters run and jump over and across logs and rocks, stopping to eye humans with curiosity. Although chipmunks are in the same family and share many characteristics with squirrels, we rarely see them climbing trees. Instead, they are categorized as a type of ground squirrel, which often sticks to the ground as they know how to masterfully navigate it.

Curious Explorations

Baby chipmunks spend their first six to eight weeks of life underground. For the first four weeks or so, it doesn't matter that everything is dark, because their eyes remain closed.

However, once their eyes open around one month of age, their curiosity begins. What might be outside the underground burrow? A young chipmunk starts exploring the tunnels connecting chambers of its burrow, and eventually it follows its curiosity up and outside.

Can you imagine seeing the sunlit world for the first time? God placed instincts into a chipmunk to know when it is time to venture into the wide, wonderful world of the forest and begin collecting food. And collect it does!

Seed Stewards

Chipmunks belong to the genus of ground squirrels known as ***Tamias***. *Tamias* comes from a Greek word meaning "steward," "treasurer," or "collector." Chipmunks, and other animals in the *Tamias* genus, have a remarkable ability to collect nuts, seeds, and other foods.

Like other rodents, chipmunks have very useful hands for holding and eating. However, their hands are small and can only carry so much, so they smartly use their mouths, which are equipped with cheek pouches, to carry food. A chipmunk's cheeks are not only enormous but they also have built-in skin pouches that act like shopping bags for carrying food. Each cheek pouch is made of elastic skin that can stretch up to three times the size of the chipmunk's head to store impressive amounts of food. But where does a chipmunk take all the food it gathers?

Adult chipmunks build their own underground burrow, including three to four storage chambers that are like food pantries. Each chamber can hold several quarts of seeds or nuts, ensuring the chipmunk always has sufficient food throughout the year.

Chipmunks busy themselves with gathering and storing food as well as staying safe from predators, often darting back to their burrow or other hidey-holes they have dug to remain safe while out and about.

Time to Explore

Go explore a wooded area and look for chipmunks. They are more active in spring, summer, and fall months, but they can also be spotted on occasion in winter when they come up from their burrows to restock supplies. Can you find one stuffing food in its cheeks? What direction does it run back toward its burrow? The chipmunk's life is one of curiosity, exploring the forest floor as it goes about its daily activities. See if it stops to see what you are up to. It may be as curious about you as you are about it!

Following Curiosity's Trail

A chipmunk's curiosity about the world outside its burrow drives it to explore and find what it needs. However, that curiosity can also get it into trouble if it wanders up to a human's picnic area and eats food that is not good for it. Have you ever thought about your own curiosity and how it can lead to either good or harm?

God has tucked curiosity inside you; it is what makes you ask great questions and look for answers. Curiosity is what inspires you to explore a new trail or ask why a creature behaves a certain way. Curiosity is simply wanting to know about or experience something we don't yet understand—it's a desire to learn, like a chipmunk who wants to discover what's outside its burrow. God designed us to learn and grow, led by our curiosity.

However, the enemy, Satan, wants to take our curiosity and use it for his evil ways. He might want to make us curious about things that go against God's will and good plan for our lives. When our curiosity wants to lead us away from God's path, perhaps to look at, watch, read, or listen to something that is not good for us, we should not follow it. Instead, we should direct our curiosity back to God's path.

If ever you feel your curiosity guiding you to explore something you're not sure is good for you or not, ask your parent, caregiver, or a trusted adult. Remember, just as a chipmunk's curiosity can guide it to good or harm, so can our curiosity. Let's always follow our curiosity to good things that grow our faith and sense of wonder.

Jeremiah 33:3 says, "Call to me and I will answer you and tell you great and unsearchable things you do not know" (NIV). These words were spoken to a specific person, Jeremiah, in unique circumstances. Still, they show us how God wants to reveal himself and his ways to us, his children. The verse before says, "This is what the LORD says, he who made the earth, the LORD who formed it and established it—the LORD is his name" (NIV). The same God who brilliantly formed and established everything on earth, including curious chipmunks, wants to reveal himself to us. We can follow our God-given curiosity to discover marvelous truths about God tucked into the mysteries of nature.

Dear God, thank you for creating us with curiosity inside our hearts and minds. May our curiosity always guide us to discover wonderful things about who you are and how you made the world and everything in it. Amen.

36
Wind

Hints of the Invisible

What Makes Wind?

Have you ever seen the wind? Maybe this seems like a trick question since wind is invisible. Wind is moving air, but what causes the air to move? This might surprise you, but the sun makes wind! The sun makes wind by warming Earth unevenly. Some places heat up faster than others, so the air above warms and rises and then cooler air moves down and rushes in to take its place. All that air moving around creates wind.

What Is Wind For?

Just like everything else in nature, God purposefully created wind. Can you think of ways wind is helpful in nature?

First, wind is refreshing. Have you ever been somewhere hot and humid? Maybe you were sweating and there was no breeze! Unmoving air can become uncomfortable, while a fresh breeze on a hot summer's day refreshes us and animals.

Second, wind disperses seeds, helping more plants to grow. God gave many plant seeds tufts of silk or other ways of being carried by the wind. Wind picks up seeds and carries them to another place so they can grow and spread.

Third, wind helps some animals travel. Birds ride on gusts of wind or soar up on hot air currents called ***thermals***. Riding the wind helps birds save energy, which can be lifesaving on their long migration journeys.

Insects and spiders also use wind to travel. Flying insects ride on the wind, and some spiders take a ride on the wind through ***ballooning***. They shoot their silk into the air, and Earth's ***electric field***, along with wind, helps them soar—even hundreds of miles!

Fourth, wind moves clouds, helping to spread rain and snow over the land and bring water to plants and animals.

Fifth, wind creates ocean waves, which help mix oxygen into the water, caring for God's marine creatures. While we're on the topic of wind helping ocean creatures, wind also creates currents on the ocean's surface that are like big roundabouts in the ocean. Many living things, from tiny sea plankton to jellyfish, eels, sea turtles, penguins, and whales, use ocean currents to travel, all thanks to wind! Just as birds in the air use the wind to save energy during their long journeys, ocean creatures use it to conserve energy during their travels.

That's a lot of amazing uses for wind! When God spoke the sun into place in Genesis 1:14, he wasn't thinking only about light and warmth. He was also thinking about how to move air around so that many creatures—and humans—can thrive.

Seeing Wind

Although we cannot see wind because it is made of invisible air, we can see what it does. If you step outside on a breezy day, what evidence do you see that the wind is at work? In spring, you might watch seeds floating through the air, carried by wind. In the summer, a butterfly might ride a breeze through your yard. In the fall, you might spot birds traveling on the wind or circling higher as they save energy by hitching a ride on thermals. In winter, wind might push snow in beautiful white sheets across your yard or cause snowdrifts to pile up so you can build a snowman or go sledding.

Some things God created we cannot see directly, like air and wind, but that does not make them any less real. We can't see wind, but we know it is there when it rustles tree leaves and refreshes us on a hot day.

Time to Explore

Step outside. How much proof can you find that the wind is blowing? Can you see it carrying seeds or pushing clouds? Can you feel the wind against your skin? Can you smell fragrances carried by the wind? Do you hear leaves rustling in the breeze? Write or draw all the evidence you can find for wind.

Hints of the Invisible

We cannot see wind, but we can glimpse it at work. In a similar way, we cannot see God's Holy Spirit, but we can watch him at work in our lives and in the world around us.

When we trust Jesus and follow him as our Savior, God's Holy Spirit comes to live inside us. He helps us every day. How does God's Holy Spirit help us?

- He teaches us and reminds us of everything Jesus said (John 14:26).
- He guides us "into all truth," helping us understand God's words (John 16:13).
- He helps us walk in God's way and not give in to temptation (Gal. 5:16).
- He helps us know how to pray and talks to God on our behalf (Rom. 8:26–27).
- He marks us as God's followers (Eph. 1:13–14).

We cannot see the Holy Spirit, but just as with wind, we can see what he does. When you notice God guiding you, helping you, answering your prayers, reminding you of truth, and protecting you, you are seeing God's Holy Spirit at work.

His Spirit is so powerful that he raised Jesus from the dead, and that same powerful Spirit is at work in us. Romans 8:11 says, "The Spirit of God, who raised Jesus from the dead, lives in you. And just as God raised Christ Jesus from the dead, he will give life to your mortal bodies by this same Spirit living within you" (NLT).

Just as you can go outside and watch the wind at work, look for the Holy Spirit moving in your life. Perhaps keep a journal of the ways you see him working.

> *Dear God, thank you for making the sun that creates wind, which refreshes us and helps nature in so many ways. Thank you for your Holy Spirit, whom we cannot see but we can glimpse at work in our lives. Help us to practice noticing your Spirit at work in and around us. Amen.*

37
Pill Bug

I Know You by Name

Tricky Identity

Has a creature ever tricked you into thinking it was something it's not? Some creatures are known for their trickery. Opossums play dead. The mimic octopus can change its shape to resemble other underwater creatures. The orchid mantis (a type of insect) looks like an orchid blossom, blending in as it waits for prey. Some creatures have special ways of tricking those around them. Other creatures don't try to fool us, but figuring out what they are can be a challenge, which is true of the pill bug.

The Problem with Nicknames

Have you ever heard of a pill bug? You might have heard it called by other names. Where I grew up in Wisconsin, we called them roly-polies. In the United States and Canada, they are also called tomato bugs, potato bugs, wood bugs, armadillo bugs, doodle bugs, carpenters, and boat-builders. That is a lot of nicknames for the same creature!

In Australia, they are called butcher boys, and in New Zealand, slaters. In the United Kingdom, this creature goes by several names: cheesy bugs, cheesy bobs, cheeselogs, chucky pig, chuggy peg, daddy grampher, crawley baker, and granny grey.

Besides the United Kingdom's cheesy theme, did you notice any other similarities in some of the nicknames? Many end in *bug*, which can be misleading because this creature is not a bug at all. Its scientific name is ***Armadillidiidae***. (I agree—cheesy bob is easier to say!)

Every living creature has been sorted into categories in science. Each specific creature has its own ***scientific name***, which helps people across the world know if they are talking about the same creature. Every creature can also have many ***common names***, which are like nicknames. As with the pill bug, nicknames can be confusing because people around the world, or even within a country, might call the same creature by different nicknames.

If Not a Bug, What Is It?

Not only is a pill bug not a bug, it's not even an insect! So what is it?

If you have ever seen or held one of these tiny creatures, you might have noticed its many legs (fourteen to be exact), or its armor-like back that makes it look a bit like an armadillo that met a shrink ray machine. The pill bug can also roll its body into a tight ball (to stay safe from predators or retain water) like some armadillos do. But these creatures are not armadillos either. They are crustaceans.

Have you ever heard the word *crustacean* or know of other animals that are part of this category? Shrimp, lobsters, crayfish, and crabs are crustaceans. The pill bug is a ***terrestrial crustacean***. *Terrestrial* refers to land, meaning they live on land rather than in the water. Pill bugs are often found beneath logs, leaves, or mulch because God gave these terrestrial crustaceans the important job of recycling dead things to create healthy soil for new plants to grow.

Think about it—*someone* needs to clean up rotting sticks, leaves, and other dead parts of plants. Otherwise, it would all pile up. God designed many small creatures, including pill bugs, to be ***decomposers***. Decomposers are nature's recycling crew. They eat dead things on the ground and turn them into nutrients for the soil so new plants can grow. It's a beautiful picture of making all things new, just like God will one day do across his beautiful creation.

Time to Explore

Go look for pill bugs in your yard or in a nearby garden. Pill bugs have ***negative phototaxis***, which means they avoid light, so they can often be found in dark areas beneath rocks, logs, and bark. Can you count all fourteen legs on one pill bug? Does it roll up into a ball when you place it in your hand? Admire how God designed the pill bug, then gently let it go on its way.

I Know You by Name

It can be hard to walk into a room where no one knows your name or who you are. One of the first things people do when they meet is share their names, but how often do we remember someone's name after they tell it to us? Sometimes it can take meeting a person a few times or spending time with them before we easily remember their name.

We feel seen and important when someone knows our name. In Isaiah 43:1, God said to the Israelites, "Don't be afraid, because I have saved you. I have called you by name, and you are mine." Although God was speaking to a specific group of people, his words give us a glimpse into his heart. Because Jesus came to offer salvation to everyone, we can be with God—we are his and he knows us by name!

When God wants to speak to us, he doesn't begin with "Hey, you over there!" No, he knows each of his children, and he calls us by name. And he also has nicknames for us, but unlike cheesy bob or chucky pig, they are not silly nicknames; they are meaningful. God calls us *beloved*, and when we follow Jesus as our Savior, he calls us *redeemed and rescued*, *forgiven*, and *free.*

If ever you feel unseen or unknown, remember that the creator of the cosmos knows and calls you by name. That's pretty marvelous!

Dear God, thank you for creating a little creature that looks like a miniature armadillo. Sometimes your creation makes us smile and laugh! Thank you for knowing and calling us by name. Help us to remember the names you have for us and that we are seen and loved by you. Amen.

38

Cattail

One Body, Many Parts

Cattail Fuzz

Have you ever taken apart a cattail and scattered its fuzz into the wind? The brown end of a cattail that resembles a hot dog is the female part of the plant, which holds the seeds. Inside the brown part is tucked a mass of soft, silky fuzz, which has been nicknamed cattail down or swamp down, because it resembles a bird's soft downy feathers. God packed cattail seedheads full of this soft, light fuzz, as it is easily carried by wind. The fuzz is attached to the seeds, and when the wind blows and catches the fuzz, it carries the seeds away to plant new cattails nearby. Each brown, sausage-shaped seedhead can hold around 220,000 seeds. Cattails are designed just right to carry out their God-given directions from Genesis 1:11, "Let the earth produce plants—some to make grain for seeds and others to make fruits with seeds in them. Every seed will produce more of its own kind of plant."

But why are cattails important?

A Plant with Many Purposes

Cattails not only create a beautiful frame around many ponds but they are also very useful to humans and creatures.

Have you ever enjoyed eating corn on the cob? Or have you made a pillow or stuffed animal? Have you ever woven something or made a basket? Have you baked a cake or enjoyed creamy soup? Cattails can be used for all of these purposes! Here are some of the many ways cattails have been used by humans:

- Immature cattail flowers (while they are still small and green) can be cooked and eaten like corn on the cob.
- Pollen from cattails can be used as a type of flour in baking or as a thickener in cooking recipes.
- A cattail's underground stems can be baked, broiled, or grilled for a tasty and unique meal.
- Cattail fuzz is helpful for stuffing pillows, stuffed animals, or sleeping bags.
- Cattail leaves can be woven into baskets, mats, or shelters.

It's not only humans that use cattails; many of God's creatures also find creative ways to make much of this plant. I love finding red-winged blackbird homes among cattails. These birds masterfully weave their nests between cattails, making use of the plant's sturdy structure. Along with using them as nesting spots, many birds also eat cattails and use their fuzz as a soft material with which to build cozy nests.

Cattails also provide safe havens in shallow water where frogs and salamanders can lay their eggs. Muskrats use cattails to construct their lodge homes, and cattails are on the menu for many animals, including beavers.

Anchored Together

Cattails do not have roots like many other plants do. Instead, they have rhizomes. Rhizomes are similar to roots because they grow underground and help anchor plants. However, they are hidden underground stems that can also store food for a plant and grow new shoots from ***growth nodes*** to help the plant spread and strengthen. Rhizomes create a strong carpet of stems that anchors cattails in the ground, keeping them sturdy and strong and growing new cattails from the same stem network.

Time to Explore

Explore a wetland area and find cattails. Is it early spring or summer when the flowers are young and green? Or is it late summer when the female flower is brown, sausage-like, and packed with fuzzy stuffing? Is it later in the season when the cattail has opened and fuzz is beginning to spill out and catch on the wind, spreading seeds? If you're in an area where you're allowed to pick plants, gather cattail leaves and try weaving a mat or a basket or making a pillow or stuffed animal with felt or fabric and stuffing it with cattail down.

One Body, Many Parts

Just as a cattail is one plant with many parts and purposes, so is the body of believers. In the Bible, the body of believers refers to everyone who loves and follows Jesus, trusting him as their Savior. There are local bodies of believers in churches and a worldwide body of believers that includes everyone who follows Jesus.

In 1 Corinthians 12:12, we read, "A person's body is one thing, but it has many parts. Though there are many parts to a body, all those parts make only one body. Christ is like that also."

Think about a cattail with its sturdy leaves, anchoring rhizome stems, flowers, fuzz, pollen, and seeds. It is one plant with many parts and purposes, just like the body of believers!

This passage continues to explain that each part of the body of believers—every person—has unique gifts and roles. It explains that just as the human hand, foot, eye, and ear all have special abilities and purposes, each follower of Christ has special giftings and jobs to do.

Think about trying to weave a basket from a cattail's fuzz—that would not work very well! Or what if you tried stuffing a pillow with a cattail's pollen instead of its fuzz? That would take forever and might make you sneeze. Every part of a cattail has special purposes, just as every follower of Jesus has unique talents and can serve God and his children in special ways.

Finally, think about a patch of cattail plants next to a pond. Picture the strong rhizome network beneath, anchoring them to the ground and each other. Similarly, God's believers are anchored together in Christ and his teachings. Ephesians 4:2–3 offers this encouragement for remaining anchored to each other, "Always be humble, gentle, and patient, accepting each other in love. You are joined together with peace through the Spirit, so make every effort to continue together in this way."

Dear God, thank you for creating cattails with so many uses. We are grateful you created us with special gifts and important work to do in the body of believers. Help us to stay anchored to other believers and to serve in the plans and purposes you have for us. Amen.

39
Fool's Gold (Pyrite)

A True Fortune

Tricky Treasure

Have you ever found something that seemed valuable at first sight but wasn't? Maybe you discovered a ring or other piece of jewelry that looked expensive, but upon closer inspection, you discovered it was made from cheap materials. What about in nature? Have you ever found something that looked like gold?

Sometimes, while exploring God's creation, my kids have found what looked like a golden nugget. Pyrite is a mineral that looks so much like gold, it's been nicknamed fool's gold. How do you think it is different from real gold?

Pyrite is a mix of minerals. It is made from both iron and sulfur. But gold is pure; it is its own element.

Think of it like mixing colors. Some colors can be mixed to make new colors. What color can you make by mixing blue and red? Purple! What color does red and yellow make? Orange! How can you make the color red? That's a trick question! Red cannot be created by other colors. Red, yellow, and blue are primary colors, which means you cannot mix other colors to make them.

Pure gold is like a primary color; you cannot mix other things to make it. Pyrite, or fool's gold, is like a mixed color. It's created by mixing two main elements—iron and sulfur.

Pyrite is also brittle and can easily be broken. But do you think you could snap a piece of gold in half? No, gold is nearly impossible to snap because it is soft and ***malleable***. It can be hammered or pressed into another shape without breaking.

Useful Fool's Gold

When it comes to price, pure gold is far more valuable than pyrite. But God made pyrite as a unique creation, and it is very useful to humans. Before matches and gas-filled lighters were invented, pyrite was used to start fires. Long ago, Vikings carried pyrite in fire-starting kits. Pyrite was an important tool for starting fires for cooking, light, and warmth.

Pyrite is also used in the production of nutritional supplements, water treatment, and paper. It is even being researched as a low-cost, nontoxic material for use in solar panels.

Pyrite is only one of the many minerals God designed. He designed minerals, and the more basic elements they are made from, to help humans invent useful things. So, if you're looking for true gold, pyrite might be a disappointment. But if you need to start a fire for warmth, pyrite is more valuable than gold!

Golden Fossils

Pyrite is both useful and beautiful. Its ***luster*** differs from that of pure gold. One example of pyrite's unique shine is ***pyritized fossils***.

If a creature dies and is rapidly covered by sand or other ***sediment***, the creature's hard bones or shell can be preserved as fossils. Many creatures were fossilized by this process during the worldwide flood described in Genesis.

Something very special happens to some fossils. If a bone or shell is buried in an area with very little oxygen and a special kind of bacteria, it can be broken down and replaced with pyrite. This creates a golden-looking fossil that's truly one of a kind.

Time to Explore

Go on a search for fool's gold. With permission or help from a trusted adult, research if there are areas with pyrite around where you live. You can also visit a rock and mineral shop to see pyrite. Notice its interesting crystalline structure.

Another mineral often mistaken for gold is mica, which is flakier than pyrite and is often found on rocks. Sunlight reflects off mica like a little mirror. Watch for the glint of fool's gold while on a trail and appreciate the beauty of God's wild and wonderful world.

A True Fortune

The Bible talks about a true fortune. It is far more valuable than gold and more useful than pyrite. Jesus told a story about this treasure in Matthew 13:44. He said, "The kingdom of heaven is like a treasure hidden in a field. One day a man found the treasure, and then he hid it in the field again. He was so happy that he went and sold everything he owned to buy that field."

Can you imagine selling everything to buy one thing? The man knew that what he had found was one of a kind. It was worth giving up everything else for. He wasn't even sad about selling what he owned. He was happy.

God's kingdom is like this. He might not call us to give up all we own. But God wants us to surrender our lives to him and offer our time, energy, thoughts, affections, and resources. When we do, he can use our lives to build his kingdom by telling others about his truth and love.

Jesus also talks about a true treasure kept in heaven. He says we can store up that treasure now. We build eternal treasure as we hide God's Word in our hearts, live according to his ways, and share his love and truth with others. It is kind of like making deposits in a bank account. Matthew 6:19–20 says, "Don't store treasures for yourselves here on earth where moths and rust will destroy them and thieves can break in and steal them. But store your treasures in heaven where they cannot be destroyed by moths or rust and where thieves cannot break in and steal them."

The enemy, Satan, wants to trick us with fool's gold. He tries to distract us from the pure treasure of God's kingdom. He entices us to chase after things like money, toys, fame, or a fancy home. Things are not bad, but if we're not careful, they can distract us from God's best for us. Instead, we can set our eyes on Jesus and growing his kingdom, which is far more valuable than gold.

Dear God, thank you for creating things as beautiful as gold and as useful as pyrite. Help us to be undistracted by earthly things and to store up treasure in heaven as we learn about you and share your truth and love with others. Amen.

40

Fog

In Plain Sight

Clouds on the Ground

Have you ever wondered what it would be like to walk on a cloud? Maybe you have traveled in an airplane and seen clouds up close. Did you know that walking outside on a foggy day is similar to walking through the clouds? Fog and clouds are made the same way. They are groups of tiny water droplets or ice crystals gathered together. Fog forms close to the Earth's surface while clouds form higher in the air.

Why do you think God made fog? What is it useful for? Remember what fog is made of—water or ice. Fog brings water to the land so more plants can grow. It is an important part of the ***water cycle***, a system God set up at creation.

The Water Cycle

When God designed water, he was thinking about how to care for all creatures and us. Psalm 104:10–11 says, "You make springs pour into the ravines; they flow between the mountains. They water all the wild animals." Have you ever seen a deer drinking from a creek? What about a bird stopping at a lake's shore to rehydrate? God created rivers, streams, lakes, and ponds to bring fresh water to animals.

Fog is another tool God uses to provide fresh water for his creations. Tiny water droplets from fog collect on plant leaves. The drops join together to make larger water droplets, which then drip down to the ground, where they can soak into the plant's roots. This is called ***fog drip***. It's like a big natural water collection system. This is especially helpful in areas with little rainfall. An area can still receive helpful moisture in the form of fog.

When God designed creation, he considered many ways to provide water for all his creatures—and for us!

Vitamin Delivery

Has your parent or caregiver ever ordered vitamins to be delivered in the mail? Fog acts as a vitamin delivery service for nature.

Sometimes, the fog droplets that collect on plants through fog drip have come from over the ocean. As that fog travels over ocean water, it can pick up salt and other minerals. Now the tiny water droplets are like little packages of minerals. When the fog moves inland, such as into the forest, the water droplets with minerals collect on plants and drip down to their roots.

God engineered so many details into the water cycle, including the delivery of minerals from the ocean to inland plants.

A Protective Hug

Fog can also act like a protective layer over certain habitats. Have you ever played in the water from a hose or gone swimming and then run to give someone a hug? If the person you run up to is dry, a wet hug might not be welcomed. Fog is like a wet hug for a natural area, but creatures and plants definitely welcome fog hugs as helpful protection.

Fog protects plants and creatures by scattering harsh sunlight. When sunlight hits the tiny water droplets in fog, it spreads light out in many directions. This is why we might not see the sun directly when it's foggy out, and the day might feel dreary or overcast even without heavy rain clouds. This scattering of light acts as a shield, protecting plants and animals from overheating or harsh UV rays.

Time to Explore

Go outside on a foggy day. Even if it doesn't look foggy in your yard, you can often find fog in the morning near or over lakes, ponds, and rivers. What does it feel like to walk through fog? Is the air hot or cold? Dry or wet? Can you see tiny water droplets collecting on plant leaves? Think about all the moisture soaking into the land and consider how God brings fresh water to his creation.

In Plain Sight

Sometimes fog can cause disappointment. If you visit a beautiful mountain or meadow, you might be sad if fog is hiding the view. Yet fog can focus our attention on the beauty right in front of us.

One day I visited a mountain stream with my family. We had been to that area many times before, and I loved the mountain view. Yet on this day, the stunning peaks were hidden by fog. At first, I was disappointed. I knew the mountains were there, but I could not enjoy them. Then I looked ahead to the creek, which was close enough to see through the fog. The willow bushes were bright red and orange, contrasting with the gray fog. The stream's water was crystal clear. The pine trees surrounding us were crisp, green, and lively, with birds jumping from branch to branch. I had never before paid such close attention to the beauty of the creek and forest.

When life feels foggy and the path ahead isn't clear, God invites us to notice the beauty and opportunities right where we are. Fog temporarily obscures what's far away so we can focus on what's near. Proverbs 4:25 says, "Keep your eyes focused on what is right, and look straight ahead to what is good."

We don't need to be frustrated when we can't see the whole path. And we don't need to be distracted by life's many big opportunities that act like mountain summits demanding our attention. Instead, we can focus on God's truth, which is always in plain sight. As we do, he'll make clear the path ahead.

Dear God, thank you for creating the water cycle with fog to bring fresh water to creation. You considered every detail. When life feels foggy and we can't see the way ahead, help us focus on what is always in sight: the truth and goodness of your Word. Amen.

41

Bear Scat

Filling Up on God's Word

Following Scat Clues

Have you ever found a wild animal's poop before? Finding a pile of animal poop, called scat, gives us clues as to what wild animals are around and what they have been up to. Recently, I found scat from black bears in three different areas. When I looked closely at a pile of bear scat (but not too closely), I saw what they had been eating. Here is where I recently found bear scat and the clues I discovered about their diet.

- Alpine wilderness: The scat was a deep blue color. There were many twinberry honeysuckle bushes growing in the area with large, dark purple berries. Many of the bushes no longer had any berries on them, leaving me to conclude the bear had most likely been eating twinberry honeysuckle berries.
- River valley: The scat looked almost crumbly and was mostly made up of small pits or seeds. In the area, there were many chokecherry plants, which are likely what the bear was snacking on.
- Next to my mailbox: The scat pile was small and filled with chunks of undigested apples. My neighbor's yard is full of apple trees with branches that bend low to the ground, heavy with fruit. Black bears often visit our neighborhood at night. Recently, we spotted a mama black bear with two cubs, around seven or eight months old, which is when they begin to eat more solid foods. I'm guessing the small pile was left by one of her cubs after visiting my neighbor's apple trees.

Readying for Winter

Toward the end of summer and through fall, I usually notice more bear scat as bears are getting ready for colder months. Contrary to popular belief, bears do not actually hibernate. Their body temperature does not lower enough to be considered a hibernating animal. However, bears do take long winter naps; this is called ***carnivore lethargy*** or ***denning***.

Before cozying up for a long winter nap, a black bear experiences something called ***hyperphagia***, which is an extreme hunger that is difficult or impossible to satisfy. If a human experiences hyperphagia and is unable to feel full from eating, it can be a sign of illness or a medical condition. However, it helps black bears store up enough fat to survive colder months.

During hyperphagia, black bears can eat up to twenty thousand calories a day. While some bears are known for eating a lot of calorie-packed meat (like polar bears and Kodiak bears), black bears mainly eat plants, including a whole lot of berries. One pound of berries might offer two hundred to three hundred calories. That means if a black bear were eating only berries, it would need to eat around eighty pounds of berries each day! Black bears will mix up their diet and enjoy nuts, insects, worms, and other small animals, but they mostly fill their bellies with berries and other plants.

God designed black bears with big paws to grab branches of berries and a long tongue to strip the branch of berries so they can quickly and efficiently gather a mouthful. I've enjoyed watching black bears meander across hillsides in the forest while foraging for berries and flipping over rocks in search of insects.

Time to Explore

Go search for animal scat. Check out from the library or purchase a guidebook or pamphlet for identifying scat around where you live, or, with permission, find a scat identification resource online. Explore a natural area and see if you can find scat clues to identify the wild animals that live there and what they have been eating.

Filling Up on God's Word

During hyperphagia, a bear's appetite is hard to satisfy. It would be challenging to work all day finding food, constantly eating, and still feeling hungry.

Do you know what it means to be ***satisfied***? To be satisfied means we are pleased and content. We have what we need and do not want or need more. To be satisfied is to have enough.

Many things on earth might promise to satisfy us, but they will always leave us hungry for more. Maybe a commercial will tell you about a product that will make you feel like you have enough, are enough, or don't need anything else. However, nothing on earth can truly satisfy us—only God can. If we reach for things like toys, video games, money, fame, or even relationships with other humans to satisfy us, we will be like a bear in hyperphagia, always hungry for more. Instead, as we reach for God's Word, we can be truly satisfied, lacking nothing we need.

In Matthew 4:4, Jesus said, "People do not live by bread alone, but by every word that comes from the mouth of God" (NLT). This verse reminds us that God's Word is what gives us true, everlasting life; it nourishes our souls.

In John 6:35, Jesus also said, "I am the bread of life. Whoever comes to me will never be hungry again" (NLT).

Can you imagine never being hungry again? In this verse, Jesus is talking about a different hunger than what makes our stomach grumble between mealtimes. This is a soul hunger. In this verse Jesus reminds us that as we follow him, we won't need to look to earthly things to fill us—they never can. Instead, he will fill up our hearts to overflowing with his goodness and love.

Dear God, thank you for creating bears to find what they need to survive winter. We are so grateful that you satisfy us with your truth and love. We never have to hunger after things in this world, because you give us all we need. Amen.

42

Beetle

Growing Up in God's Plan

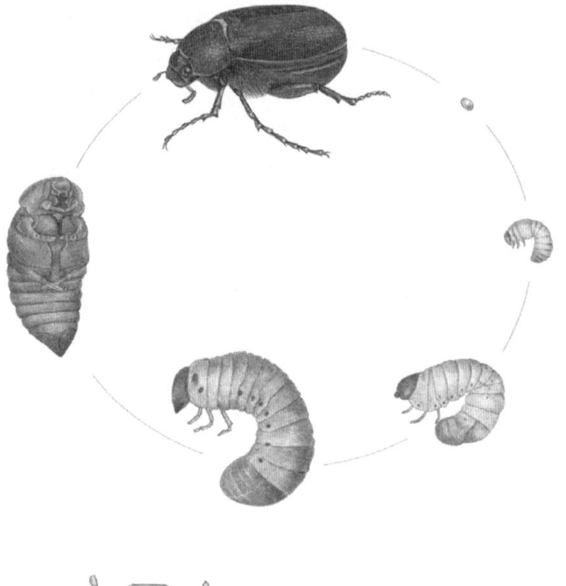

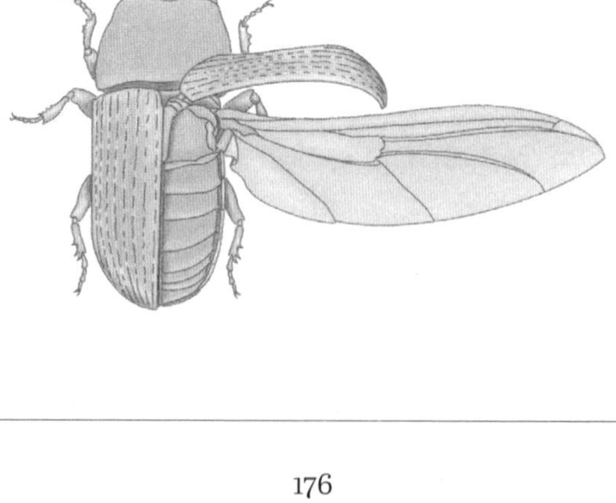

Countless Designs

Have you ever found a beetle in your yard or on a nature walk? Some beetles catch our attention because they are shiny. They come in many different colors and patterns. Can you remember any beetles you have found? What colors were they?

There are around 350,000 recognized types of beetles in the world. But scientists believe the number of types might be closer to one to two million! Only God knows the exact number of beetles he has made. Take a moment to picture God back when he was creating everything. Hebrews 11:3 tells us God created everything out of nothing. God invented every color, and then he used those colors to design everything in creation, including each type of beetle. That is a lot of designs! Although each beetle is unique, they do share many things in common, including how they grow up.

A Growing Beetle

Does a baby beetle look like its parents? Not at all! Beetles grow up through a process called metamorphosis. You might have heard of metamorphosis if you learned how caterpillars turn into butterflies. Almost all insects, including beetles, go through metamorphosis. Let's look closely at how a beetle grows up:

A beetle begins in an egg laid by a mother beetle.

The beetle hatches, becoming a larva, which looks like a small worm or grub with short legs. It does not look like a beetle at all!

As the beetle larva grows, it sheds its ***exoskeleton***, or outer shell.

When it is ready to become an adult beetle, the larva enters its ***pupal state***, where its outer shell protects it as it grows into an adult beetle.

The adult beetle emerges from the pupa with wings, and it's able to fly for the first time.

Just as you outgrow your old clothes, a young beetle outgrows its exoskeleton and grows a new, larger one.

What do you think a beetle experiences as it grows up? Beetles do not feel or experience emotions in the way we do. They simply follow God's design that is engineered into their bodies. And that plan is quite marvelous!

Beetle Armor

God gave beetles exactly what they need to be protected as they grow up. Beetles do not have skin to protect them like we do, and they also do not have a skeleton inside to help give them shape and support. Instead, God designed beetles with a protective covering that acts like armor to protect the beetle's soft tissues and wings. It is called an exoskeleton because it is on the outside of its body.

Two Sets of Wings

Adult beetles have wings. And think about this: God engineered the design for those wings into the tiny beetle egg and larva. When the adult beetle emerges from its pupa, it is not a new kind of creature. It is the creature God always designed it to be; the beetle has simply grown up into God's plan, and that great plan includes careful protection for its important wings.

Have you ever heard of a beetle's ***elytra***? The elytra are the hard outer forewings we see on a beetle when it is climbing or walking. The elytra of some species are brightly colored, shiny, and have patterns on them, making many beetles the jewels of nature! The elytra are not only pretty but they also protect the hindwings inside, which are much more delicate and are used for flight. God thought of everything each kind of beetle would need, and he programmed the instructions for them into a tiny beetle egg.

Time to Explore

Go on a beetle search! You can identify a beetle because its shiny elytra meet and form a line down the middle of its back. Look at plant leaves, stems, and flowers, and at tree trunks. How many different types of beetles can you find? Try sketching some in a notebook using colored pencils to match their brilliant colors. Can you find a beetle taking off in flight? See if you can spot both its protective coverings and delicate hindwings while it's in the air.

Growing Up in God's Plan

Do you ever feel like growing up is hard? Perhaps you've been given more responsibility recently or there are new challenges to face. Getting older can be both exciting and difficult.

Beetles don't experience growing up in the same ways we do. Baby beetles don't look forward to having wings one day, like you might be excited to learn how to drive. And beetles don't have to figure out how to handle challenging situations with friends or be faithful in a new task or responsibility. They face their own challenges, such as finding food and shelter.

However, we can learn a lot from the way a beetle grows up. It cannot see the future or know what it will be like to one day be a shiny adult with wings, maneuvering through the sky. It simply grows up following God's design and plan. And we can do the same.

In Matthew 6:34, Jesus said, "So don't worry about tomorrow, because tomorrow will have its own worries." We do not have to worry about the future or the challenges we'll face as we get older. Like a beetle, we can follow the plan God created for us and grow up into his purposes. And unlike a beetle, we can deeply rely on God as we grow up into those plans. A beetle grows up by instinct, or how God created it to, but we can grow up in deep faith because we have an everlasting spirit that was created to have a relationship with God. Philippians 4:6–7 offers this encouragement, "Do not worry about anything, but pray and ask God for everything you need, always giving thanks. And God's peace, which is so great we cannot understand it, will keep your hearts and minds in Christ Jesus."

We can fully trust God in every uncertainty and challenge as we grow up into his great plan.

Dear God, thank you for giving beetles what they need to grow up. You have amazing plans for our lives. Help us to trust you in every hard thing as we grow up into your plan, learning more about you and spending time in prayer. Amen.

43
Fern

Order from Chaos

A Feather-Shaped Plant

What are some of your favorite shapes to find in nature? Do you enjoy spotting the spiral in a snail's shell or the sharp points of deer antlers? Have you ever seen a hexagon in a bee's honeycomb? God filled his wonderful creation with all kinds of circles, squares, hexagons, spirals, and other shapes for us to marvel at. Some of his fun shapes can be seen in the design of a fern plant.

Have you ever seen a fern? Ferns are green plants that grow from the ground on long stems. Each long stem has many soft, feathery leaves on both sides. One entire fern leaf is called a ***frond***, and it is shaped like a bird feather. The smaller-looking leaves sticking out on either side are called ***pinnae***, and those leaves are made of even tinier parts.

Imagine a fern frond as a long green feather. The main stem of the frond is like the feather's tough, supportive quill, and the leaflet pinnae are like one piece of the feather. Even the pinnae, which look like leaves to us, are made of even smaller leaflike parts called ***pinnules***. Pinnules are usually small, narrow, and oval- or teardrop-shaped. Don't worry about memorizing the names of the fern parts (unless you want an extra challenge). Right now, just marvel at the incredible details and shapes God used when he invented this fun plant.

Ferns remind us that as we zoom in and look closer at nature, we see many more detailed designs and the artistic style of our creative God.

Repeating Patterns in Nature

The shapes in ferns are not only beautiful but also very mathematical. They are ***fractals***, which means the design of their leaves repeats again and again at different sizes—big, medium, and tiny.

When we look at a fern frond, we see a large plant shaped like a feather. As we zoom in, we see the pinnae on each side, which resemble small feathers. Looking even closer at the pinnules, we see even smaller feather-like shapes.

For a long time, scientists believed that shapes in nature were random and chaotic. Many things didn't fit into clean, tidy categories of circles, squares, and hexagons. In 1982, a mathematician named Benoît Mandelbrot discovered and named repeating patterns (like we see in ferns) fractals. Now we understand that shapes that might seem messy actually have incredible design and order. Ferns are that way. When my family walks through the Redwood forests in California, ferns carpet the forest floor. Their leaves shoot out in every direction and sometimes look like a tangled mess. However, upon closer inspection, we find that ferns are not messy at all. They are exactly as God designed them—unique and beautiful!

Fiddlehead Spirals and Spore Circles

Ferns do not begin their lives shaped like a feather. When the fern frond begins growing up from the ground, it is called a ***fiddlehead***, and it is coiled up like a spiral. They are named fiddleheads because the curled-up fern looks like the spiral shape at the end of a violin or fiddle.

The spiral shape of a fern fiddlehead is a very special shape in nature called a ***Fibonacci spiral***. Along with ferns, the Fibonacci spiral can be seen in a seahorse's curled tail, pine cones, sunflower heads, the shape of hurricanes and galaxies, snail shells, and in many other creations God made. Creation's spirals show us God's style throughout nature.

There are two more important shapes in ferns we should mention: circles and ovals. Tiny brown circles or ovals can often be found on the underside of fern fronds. These are called ***sporangia***, and they help the fern reproduce to make more ferns. Ferns do not make flowers or seeds like many other plants. Instead, they produce tiny spores, much like mushrooms make spores. A fern's spores are tucked into the sporangia, which are like packets of spores. The sporangia packets release the spores, which are carried by the wind to a new area where more ferns can grow.

From feather-shaped fronds and leaves to spiral fiddleheads and circle spore packets, ferns are smartly engineered using math and shapes.

Time to Explore

Observe a fern from about ten feet away. Can you sketch the shape of it? After a while, move to a distance of five feet away. Do you notice any more details in the pinnae leaves? Now, move right next to the fern. Can you see the smaller feather patterns in the individual parts of the leaf? Notice how the smaller parts resemble the larger parts and check under the fern for spore packets.

Order from Chaos

Sometimes life feels messy. Maybe we don't know what decisions to make or why a hard thing is happening. It's easy to feel like the circumstances around us are out of control and do not make any sense. However, when we feel this way, we can remember that God is not a God of confusion or chaos. Instead, he is a God of order and peace (see 1 Cor. 14:33).

Remember a fern's many feather-like shapes, from its large fronds to the smaller pinnae and pinnules. Each part shows order and a repeating pattern. The same God who designed ferns knows every big and small detail of our lives. Psalm 139:1–6 says:

> LORD, you have examined me
>   and know all about me.
> You know when I sit down and when I get up.
>   You know my thoughts before I think them.
> You know where I go and where I lie down.
>   You know everything I do.
> LORD, even before I say a word,
>   you already know it.
> You are all around me—in front and in back—
>   and have put your hand on me.
> Your knowledge is amazing to me;
>   it is more than I can understand.

From the beginning of time God has created order and purpose in nature, and we can watch him do the same in our lives.

Things on earth, stories in the news, or situations in our lives can feel chaotic because we live on a planet that is cursed by sin. However, God's plan is bigger than any darkness. God has defeated sin and death, and he will one day make all things new. When the big picture looks messy—like a forest of tangled ferns—look closer. God is working in the details.

Dear God, thank you for creating order and purpose. Nature reveals your smart designs and reminds us we can trust you in every detail, big and small. Amen.

44
Termite

Amazing Architects

Unwanted Guests

Termites are no one's favorite insect to find, especially if they're in or around a home. Their habit of eating wood gets them into trouble. They can eat through wood in homes and other buildings, causing extensive damage and making structures unsafe.

Termites eat wood because it has a lot of cellulose, a material in plants that termites need. It's unfortunate when they decide to get that cellulose from human-made structures instead of in their natural habitat in the wild. Cellulose in wood is too tough for most creatures to eat, but termites have the help of tiny living things called ***protozoa*** in their gut that help break down the tough cellulose.

But what good did God create termites for? What is their purpose in nature? Termites are a great example of community working together, and of building things excellently. Let's look at both termite qualities.

It Takes a Village . . . or a Termite Colony

Have you ever heard someone say "It takes a village"? This saying usually refers to raising children and means that it takes many people—parents, grandparents, aunts and uncles, friends, teachers, and pastors—to help children grow up and learn. It's a picture of the power of community. Termites are another great example of a community working together.

A group of termites is called a ***colony***. Drywood termites that live only in wood can have a few thousand termites in their colony. Subterranean termites that live in the soil can have hundreds of thousands to even one million termites in their colony. That's a massive village!

Like ants, a termite colony has distinct ***castes*** or ranks. There are ***reproductives***, the future kings and queens of new colonies, who mate in flight. Similar to ants, the female removes her wings after the mating flight and begins laying eggs. Those eggs hatch into new termites for the colony. The new termites fall into three other rankings:

- Workers build the termite mound and tend to the queen.
- Soldiers defend the colony against intruders.

- Secondary reproductives serve as a backup if the queen or king dies, and they can take over egg laying so the colony can continue to grow.

These special roles ensure the termites stay safe, grow their colony by hatching more eggs, and continue ongoing building projects.

Blind Yet Masterful Builders

Speaking of building the termite mound, the workers who excavate tunnels, eat wood, and build and repair the nest area do so all without sight. Worker termites lack eyes, yet they are able to construct structures that rival human-made buildings.

Termite mounds might not look like a fancy castle or a stunning stone-built church with stained glass windows, but they are efficient. An efficient building saves energy, keeps people comfortable, and uses what's already around it—like sunlight, wind, and shade—to do the job.

Humans work hard to build efficient homes with solar energy and insulation, and some are even partly underground to maintain consistent temperatures. Termites know how to do this—without sight. Using simple materials including dirt, saliva (spit), and their own poop, they build complex tunnels and chimney systems that keep the mound cool during the day and warm at night.

Termites are so good at building efficient mounds that architects built a shopping center in Zimbabwe, Africa, inspired by termite construction to keep the building cool through its design rather than adding an expensive air-conditioning system. The termite-inspired construction saves 90 percent in energy costs compared to similar buildings. That's a smart design, and it all comes from God's smartly designed master builders: termites.

Time to Explore

Are there termite mounds near where you live? If so, go watch them at work. If not, try to find an anthill or mound. Can you see the insects working hard to build their home and care for their colony? Make up a story, song, or poem about the termite or ant workers doing their specific jobs.

Amazing Architects

What do you enjoy building? Perhaps you like building forts, tree houses, or lean-tos from sticks and branches. Or maybe you like to create with blocks, clay, or popsicle sticks. God made you to build. He is creative and makes marvelous things, and we are created in his image. You are made to be a maker!

There are some very important building projects in the Bible. Can you think of any? Here are some historical events where God told his people to build something:

- Noah built the ark to save his family from the worldwide flood.
- Moses built the tabernacle as a movable place for the Israelites to worship and sacrifice to God.
- King Solomon had a temple constructed as a central and stationary place of worship.
- Jerusalem's city walls were built and rebuilt.

When Moses and the Israelites constructed the tabernacle, God supplied an amazing artist and worker named Bezalel. Bezalel's creativity and skills did not come from his own abilities but from God.

In Exodus 31:3–5, God said this about Bezalel: "I have filled him with the Spirit of God, with wisdom, with understanding, with knowledge and with all kinds of skills—to make artistic designs for work in gold, silver and bronze, to cut and set stones, to work in wood, and to engage in all kinds of crafts" (NIV).

Like Bezalel's God-given talents, and a termite's God-given instincts and abilities to build without sight, God has tucked creativity and abilities in you. As you build and create, you can grow skills that will bring glory to God as you make things that magnify and point others to him.

Dear God, thank you for making termites excellent builders. May they always show us your intelligence in their design by working together and building energy-saving structures. Help us to use the creativity you gave us to build good things that bless others and make you smile. Amen.

45
Petrichor

A Promise of Life

The Smell of Rain

Have you ever walked outside after a spring rain? What words would you use to describe how it smelled? Sweet, earthy, or like dirt? The smell after rain falls is called petrichor (pronounced PEH-truh-kor). But why do you think nature smells a certain way after rain? It's definitely not the same as your hair smelling like shampoo after a bath or a car smelling like soap after a car wash. Instead, rain helps release different chemicals from plants and the soil into the air, where they enter our nostrils. Our brain recognizes these chemicals as the smell of the earth soaking up water. Let's look closer at the special perfume a rainfall creates and how plant oils and bacteria help mix up the wonderful smell of rain.

Plant Oils

You might not smell petrichor after every rain. It's most noticeable when rain falls after a stretch of dry days. If there are many dry days in a row, some plants will protect themselves by creating oils. This is why some plant leaves look shiny; they are covered in protective oil that helps the plant hold in moisture and stay safe from the sun's harsh rays, like a natural sunscreen. Some of these oils can also help the plant slow down its growth or press pause on making seeds. The plant might need to save energy if there is not a lot of water available. This is a special way God designed plants to grow at the right pace to protect themselves during dry seasons.

When leaves or other parts of plants fall to the ground, or when plants shed tiny amounts of these oils, the oils don't just disappear. Over time, they build up on the dirt, rocks, and sidewalks around the plants, almost like a thin invisible layer.

When it finally rains after a dry time, the raindrops splash onto these oily layers. The water stirs up tiny molecules from the oils, mixes them with other smells in the soil, and sends them into the air.

Bacteria in the Soil

Tiny living things called bacteria live in soil, and some of those bacteria make a special mixture of chemicals called ***geosmin***, which means "earth smell." Certain types of bacteria create geosmin as they carry out the work God gave them. They break down dead and decaying things in nature, helping to recycle the soil and keep it healthy so more plants can grow. When rain falls on the soil, it releases the geosmin chemicals into the air.

God designed our noses to be very sensitive to geosmin. It's estimated that a human could smell geosmin in five parts per trillion, which would be like finding a few drops of something in an Olympic-size swimming pool. Why do you think God made us to smell geosmin so well? Maybe because he wants us to inhale the earthy scent of soil and remind us he is the bringer of new life.

Time to Explore

The next time it rains, walk outside right after the rain stops and sniff the air. See if you can smell petrichor. Does it smell sweet, earthy, or like dirt? If you have a stretch of dry days, track how long you go without rainfall and then mark when the rain does come. Do this over the course of a few weeks, and record what rainfalls produce the strongest petrichor smell. Does a longer stretch of dry days create a stronger scent? Why might that be?

As you inhale, think of the plant oils and bacteria hard at work making the perfume of rainfall.

A Promise of Life

The smell of petrichor is a beautiful reminder of new life. God designed rainfall to coax plants to sprout, grow, bud, bloom, and produce seeds and fruit. Rainfall and plants can remind us of the work God's Word does in our hearts. Isaiah 55:10–11 says:

> Rain and snow fall from the sky
>   and don't return without watering the ground.
> They cause the plants to sprout and grow,
>   making seeds for the farmer
>   and bread for the people.
> The same thing is true of the words I speak.
>   They will not return to me empty.
> They make the things happen that I want to happen,
>   and they succeed in doing what I send them to do.

What does this passage say rain produces? Rainfall causes plants to sprout and grow. Plants provide much-needed food for animals and humans. God designed rainfall to grow all the plants we need.

What does this passage say God's Word produces? Just like rainfall brings forth life, God's Word waters our hearts and brings forth new life in our spirits. It always produces what God wants it to. Just as you might enjoy running outside and splashing in puddles when it's raining, we should soak ourselves in God's Word so it can consistently produce life in our hearts and minds.

Dear God, thank you for the wonderful smell of rainfall. We are so glad you designed plants with their protective oils and bacteria to recycle the soil and that you made each of these to mix up the perfume of rainfall. Whenever we smell petrichor, help us remember how you bring new life to the land and in our hearts. Amen.

46
Owl
Living Wisely

Two Truths and a Lie

Have you ever heard of the game Two Truths and a Lie? Each person shares three things about themself (two true, one false) and then the group has to guess which two things are true and which one is made-up.

Let's play the game with owls. Which of the two following statements do you believe are true about owls? Which one is false?

- Owls make almost no noise while flying.
- Many species of owls have uneven (crooked) ears.
- Owls can turn their heads all the way around.

Do you have your guess or did you already know which statement is false?

It is true that owls can fly silently because God designed their feathers like a jagged comb, breaking up the air as it moves over the wings, so they do not make a "whoosh" sound like other birds do.

It is also true that God designed many types of owls with uneven ears—one is higher than the other—giving owls excellent hearing. The sound of a scurrying mouse hits their ears a split second apart, which helps them figure out exactly where their next meal is.

It is not true that owls can turn their heads all the way around, but they can turn them nearly 270 degrees (that's almost three-fourths of the way around), which is impressive! But how do they do it?

Head-Turning Owls

God designed humans with seven ***neck vertebrae*** (bones). With that many, we can turn our heads ninety degrees to either side (one hundred and eighty degrees total).

God gave most owls fourteen vertebrae in their necks—twice as many as we have. This means an owl can turn its head far enough to see directly behind itself, and even further.

God also thought of how to keep blood flowing to their brain, even with all the head turning. An owl's neck has ***arteries***, which are tubes that carry oxygen-rich blood from the heart to the rest of the body.

Have you ever turned a garden hose on, then pinched the hose tube together to kink it and stop the water flow? Well, when an owl twists its neck, it needs to avoid kinking the arteries inside, which would keep blood with oxygen from the brain. Thankfully, God made sure an owl's blood vessels and arteries can stand up to all the owl's head twisting without getting kinked or pinched shut.

First, their arteries have extra cushioning around them so they are not easily pinched. But if an owl twists its neck in an extreme way, and an artery happens to get pinched and cannot allow blood through as well, God designed two emergency systems: (1) back routes called ***anastomoses*** (pronounced uh-nas-tuh-MOH-sees), which are smaller blood vessels that can reroute blood between arteries if one happens to get restricted and (2) small blood storage spots near the brain, like tiny tanks with an emergency supply of blood.

So while owls cannot turn their heads all the way around, their necks are well designed for twisting and bending so they can stay safe from predators and find what they need.

Are Owls Wise?

We already dispelled one owl myth; let's do another. Owls are often portrayed as being wise. Ancient Greeks used owls as a symbol of wisdom, and owls often serve as wise characters in stories. But are they wise?

Animals, including owls, do not have wisdom. They can be intelligent or smart, which is often why people say they are wise, but being smart is different from being wise.

Owls are intelligent hunters. They use their God-given abilities, including keen sight and hearing and silent flight, to find prey. They learn their hunting territory well and time their attacks just right. God created owls to be smart and find what they need. Owls gather information through their senses and use it to find prey, which is smart. It makes more sense to call owls smart than to call them wise.

Time to Explore

Go on an owl drive. Ask a parent or trusted adult to take you on a drive through a forested area at dusk when owls are most active. Drive slowly and look for the silhouette or shape of an owl on a branch. My family often drives the same route, and we have learned which trees owls frequent. We've learned the shape of the trees and quickly notice when there is a different shape—that of an owl on a branch. One evening, we found five great horned owls!

Living Wisely

How is being smart different from being wise? Proverbs 2:6 says, "Only the LORD gives wisdom; he gives knowledge and understanding." This verse talks about both knowledge and wisdom.

Knowledge is gathering facts, such as learning how many vertebrae there are in an owl's neck. Wisdom is deeper. It has to do with how we use all those facts we have gathered up. It involves sound judgment—thinking critically, really looking at the facts, and considering what they mean.

So, while animals, including owls, can be very smart, they do not have wisdom. Here's an example:

- An owl smartly gathers information about where prey is through its keen hearing and sight. (knowledge)
- An owl does not consider, "Should I share this mouse with the owl I saw yesterday?" or "What is the right thing to do in this situation?" (wisdom)

An owl gathers facts and acts by instinct.

Wisdom comes from God, and it is unique to humans. With our brains, we can gain knowledge, and with our souls, we can live wisely. God created our brains and souls to work together in harmony, beautifully using knowledge and wisdom together. God even promises to give us wisdom when we ask for it. James 1:5 says, "But if any of you needs wisdom, you should ask God for it. He is generous to everyone and will give you wisdom without criticizing you."

Dear God, thank you for creating owls to fill the dusk hour with wonder. Thank you for giving us wisdom when we ask for it. Help us to keep learning more about your marvelous creation and to live wisely according to your Word. Amen.

47
Firefly

Living Light

Light-Up Beetles

Have you ever seen a creature light up? When I was growing up in Wisconsin, summer evenings offered beautiful light shows in our yard and the fields around our neighborhood as fireflies (sometimes called lightning bugs) took flight and lit up the skies with their built-in lanterns.

Although they are called fireflies or lightning bugs, they are neither a fly nor a bug. Fireflies are a type of beetle. Like other beetles, they hatch from eggs as babies (larvae), then enter a pupal stage and emerge as adults with wings for flying. What's interesting about a firefly's life cycle is that in many species, the baby larva and protective pupa give off light, just as the adult beetle will.

Adult fireflies create flashes of light—like light shows in the evening sky—to attract mates. But why might they glow as larvae, before they are ready to mate? Many scientists believe firefly larvae glow to warn predators not to eat them, similar to how some creatures are brightly colored to signal to predators, "Hey, I'm toxic!" or "I don't taste good. Find another snack."

Whatever the reasons (and perhaps some we have not yet discovered), they are a beautiful image of light shining in the darkness.

Beetle Bodies

A firefly's "lamp," or the part of its body that gives light, is on its abdomen. If you find a beetle or look at a picture of one, can you point to the abdomen? God designed different beetle types with many tiny pieces that work together. They are designed wonderfully! And in each type of beetle, we can quickly identify three main parts of the body by looking closely: the head, ***thorax***, and abdomen.

The head is obvious. It is where we find the beetle's eyes, mouth, and antennae.

The thorax is the middle part of the beetle's body. This is where its six legs and wings are attached.

The abdomen is the part of the beetle that is behind the head and thorax. In many types of beetles, including the firefly, the abdomen is the largest part of the beetle. It holds important organs for breathing, digesting food, and laying eggs. It's usually made of several segments and is partly covered by the hard wing covers.

If you were to turn over a firefly and look at the underside of its abdomen (what we might think of as its belly), you'd see a yellow-colored lamp. But how do fireflies' lamps give off light?

Turning On the Light

A firefly is not plugged into a wall outlet (thankfully, because that would get in the way of flying!). It also doesn't have a battery pack or a light bulb, so how does it light up? God designed fireflies and some other creatures with a phenomenon called ***bioluminescence*** (pronounced bye-o-loom-in-ESS-enz). That's a big word! Let's break it into two smaller words:

- *bio* refers to life or living things
- *luminescence* means light

Bioluminescence is when a living thing makes its own light. A firefly doesn't flip a light switch on to flicker in the sky. Instead, it does a little chemistry experiment, mixing two things inside its abdomen: The first is a molecule called ***luciferin*** and the second is an enzyme called ***luciferase***. Mixing these two things creates a flash of energy that we see as the firefly's flickering light.

A firefly's light is far more efficient than lights humans have invented. God designed the firefly so that almost all the energy used to make its glow becomes light instead of heat, and almost no energy is lost as heat. If humans could discover how to create a similar light, it would save a lot of money in energy costs. God's designs are brilliant!

Time to Explore

In the summertime, if you live in an area with fireflies, visit a field or grassy area near dusk to see if you can spot them flickering.

If it's not summertime, or fireflies don't live near you, ask for permission and help to learn about another living thing that has bioluminescence, perhaps jellyfish, anglerfish, or glowing mushrooms. How do these living organisms use light?

Living Light

Can you think of where we see light in God's creation? Along with enjoying a firefly's light show, we enjoy light in sunrises and sunsets and stars, as well as the feeling of the sun warming our skin. Light allows us to see all of God's wonders.

Light is also powerful in Scripture. The first time God speaks in Scripture is in Genesis 1:3 when he says, "Let there be light." And God did not only create light—he *is* light! First John 1:5 says, "God is light, and in him there is no darkness at all."

Like fireflies, God made us to give light to the world around us. Also like fireflies, our light comes from God. He didn't design our bodies to create living light like creatures with bioluminescence, but he wants to live inside us and create light in our spirits that we can share with those we come into contact with.

Second Corinthians 4:6 says, "God once said, 'Let the light shine out of the darkness!' This is the same God who made his light shine in our hearts by letting us know the glory of God that is in the face of Christ." When we follow Jesus as our Savior, God's light shines inside our hearts, and it is not hidden. Matthew 5:14–16 tells us, "You are the light that gives light to the world. . . . And people don't hide a light under a bowl. They put it on a lampstand so the light shines for all the people in the house. In the same way, you should be a light for other people. Live so that they will see the good things you do and will praise your Father in heaven."

Let's let God's living light shine brightly through us so those around us can see his truth, goodness, and love.

Dear God, you didn't only make beetles with beautiful colors and patterns, but you made some to light up! We marvel at your endless creativity. Thank you for coming into our hearts and for creating living light inside us. Help us to shine your light brightly for others to see. Amen.

48

Mouse

Remember the Way

Which Way?

Have you ever forgotten how to get somewhere? Maybe you have only visited a place, such as a school or church, once or twice and you cannot remember where a classroom is. Or maybe you are visiting a new friend's house and need to learn where the restroom or kitchen is. After visiting a place a few times, we usually figure out which paths or hallways lead where.

When you move from one room to another in your home, you probably never think about which way to turn. You have memorized where everything is, and you can navigate without having to remember each move.

Mice are very good at learning how to get places. They can learn and memorize routes and easily retrace steps. Scientists have studied how mice navigate, and they've discovered some excellent maze-solving abilities. Researchers have placed mice in 3D mazes and tracked how they explore, find rewards, and learn the best routes through the maze. By watching mice closely and recording their behavior, scientists have unlocked secrets of mouse navigation and memory.

Mice can use two strategies to find their way: ***egocentric*** and ***allocentric navigation***. Let's look at both methods.

How Many Lefts Was That?

Have you ever retraced your steps by remembering how many right or left turns you took to get somewhere? That is an example of using egocentric navigation. A mouse uses this form of navigation by remembering how many turns it took and what direction. It is based on the mouse's location and direction rather than on what it sees around itself. This method reveals how God designed mice to think both backward and forward. Mice can recall how many turns they have taken and use that information to create a mental map. The mental map is constantly updated with every mouse move. The next time a mouse is placed in the same maze or area, it can think forward to plan the best possible route to its desired destination.

Where Is North?

Sometimes we use objects around us to help us know which direction to move in. You might remember a particular park bench to turn at to reach the playground, or you might know that a certain tree on a path marks where to turn toward home. These are called landmarks and using them to navigate is how allocentric navigation works.

I live near the Rocky Mountains, and when I am driving somewhere in town, I always know which direction is west because the mountains are to the west. By looking at where the mountains are, I know east is the opposite direction, and I can also find which roads lead north and south.

Landmark-driven allocentric navigation is another strategy mice use to move about. Along with finding their way based on their own body's location and direction, they rely on their environment and the objects around them, using both to create a mental map of their surroundings.

Master Navigators

A mouse doesn't have to choose one navigation strategy or the other; it can use both at the same time or switch between them. God engineered mice with smart brains and excellent ***spatial memory***, which allows them to remember where things are and how to get around. Using their excellent way-finding skills, they can escape predators, such as a house cat, and find the food they need.

Time to Explore

Watch a mouse navigating. Mice can be found in fields or grassy areas as well as in the woods. Can you spot a mouse finding its way along the forest floor or through tall grass? If you notice mice around your neighborhood, observe them and see if they follow the same routes over time. Can you map out a mouse's route in a sketchbook?

If you don't find a real mouse to observe, draw a pretend route a mouse might take and include things like a grassy field, a barn shed, and a stack of hay.

Remember the Way

Just as God designed mice to remember specific routes, God encourages us to make mental maps through the Bible. Mice memorize paths to retreat to safety and find what they need. Similarly, we can memorize Scripture so we can quickly find our way to God's protection and promises. Joshua 1:8 says, "Study this Book of Instruction continually. Meditate on it day and night so you will be sure to obey everything written in it. Only then will you prosper and succeed in all you do" (NLT). The word in this verse translated as *meditate* can mean to study and think deeply about something. As we read, study, and memorize Scripture, we create a mental map of God's Word. We can remember where certain things in the Bible are located more quickly and make connections between verses.

Don't be discouraged if you're not yet comfortable using the Bible. If you don't know where certain books of the Bible are or how to use chapters and verse numbers, remember that learning God's Word is a lifelong journey. Like a mouse memorizing a maze, the more time we spend navigating God's Word, the more comfortable and familiar we become with it.

Remember how mice carry a mental map inside themselves to guide them. God's Word serves as a map for us, and we can carry it in our minds and hearts. God designed our brains to memorize Scripture and our hearts to hold its truths inside. Start today by memorizing a landmark in Scripture, Psalm 32:8: "The Lord says, 'I will make you wise and show you where to go. I will guide you and watch over you.'"

Dear God, thank you for making mice such expert maze solvers. Help us practice navigating your Word, the Bible, and memorize our way through it. Amen.

49

Catfish

Super Senses

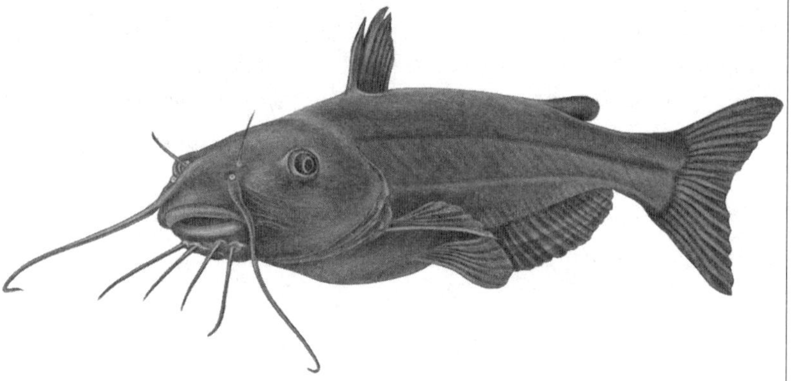

God's Gift of Senses

Have you ever sat somewhere and closed your eyes, only listening to what was around you? Or have you been blindfolded in a game, then made to smell something and guess what it was? God gave us different senses, or ways to know what is around us—smell, sight, touch, taste, and hearing. If we turn off one of those senses, such as by closing our eyes, we can focus more on another sense, like hearing or smell, and perhaps practice making it stronger.

When I guide hikes with children, I'll sometimes ask them to close their eyes for a minute and tell me what they hear. This helps them learn to listen closely. God gave us senses to explore and enjoy his wonderful world and to stay safe. God also gave creatures senses, and some even have super senses, like the catfish.

"Whiskers" for Tasting

A catfish is nicknamed for its catlike whiskers, which are called ***barbels***. What do you think their barbels are made for? Like a cat's whiskers, barbels help catfish sense what is around them, especially in the dark, murky waters they often swim in. But how the barbels are used might be surprising: They are covered in taste buds that help them find food. In fact, a catfish has taste buds all over its body! If the same were true of us, you could hold a cookie and taste it through your hand. Imagine that!

Catfish are sometimes nicknamed swimming tongues because of all those taste buds. Just as we might follow a smell to find food, catfish follow a taste as their skin and barbels detect flavors around them.

Super Smellers

Along with gifting them phenomenal tasting skills, God also gave catfish an incredible sense of smell. Inside their nostrils are tiny, folded-up structures called ***olfactory rosettes***. It's kind of like a crinkled ribbon covered in tiny sensors. As water moves into the nostril and over the ribbon, chemical compounds (like tiny packets of smell) touch the tiny sensors and send more information to the catfish's brain.

Amplified Hearing

Next time you are swimming, put your head underwater for a moment and see what you can hear. It seems like we hear less underwater, especially if we're at a busy pool with lots of kids laughing and playing above the water's surface.

But when we go underwater, everything becomes quiet. For catfish, the underwater world is not exactly quiet. God gave catfish a unique way of hearing tiny movements in the water so they can find other catfish, locate food, and avoid predators so they don't become food.

God strung an extra set of tiny bones, called a ***Weberian apparatus***, that connects a catfish's swim bladder to its inner ear, where tiny vibrations or movements turn into information the brain can use. The swim bladder helps it float and swim.

Why connect a swim bladder to the inner ear? The swim bladder works like an amplifier, making sounds stronger and louder. You can think of it as a tiny drum. When sound waves move through the water, the catfish's swim bladder starts to vibrate (or shake). These vibrations travel through the special Weberian apparatus, making them louder so the fish can hear even quiet noises around it.

We might think God gave catfish these super senses because they cannot see well, but that's not true. Along with a body covered in taste buds, nostrils full of smell sensors, and amplified hearing, catfish also have great sight. God gave them everything necessary to navigate murky waters and find what they need.

Time to Explore

Look for creatures using their senses. Can you see a rabbit twitching its nose to smell the air? Or a hawk flying overhead, using its sharp vision to scan the ground for a snack? Or ants using their specially made antennae to touch things to figure out what and who is around them?

Try to strengthen one of your senses. In a safe place outside, sit down and close your eyes for two minutes. What do you hear and smell? Are any animals chattering in the branches above? Does your nose sense any flowers or pine trees nearby? Can your skin feel the sun's warmth or a cool breeze?

Enjoy creation through all your senses and marvel at how God designed animals like catfish to experience the world in different ways.

Super Senses

God designed us with incredible senses so we can enjoy his world. Because Earth is broken by sin's curse, sometimes senses don't work as well or at all. In that case, God made it so one sense can become stronger, helping a person who cannot see to hear better, or a person who cannot hear to use touch or sight to navigate.

A woman named Helen Keller lived long ago, and an illness left her blind and deaf before she turned two years old. We might think it would be impossible to learn how to talk and communicate with others if we cannot see or hear, but Helen learned to use touch to communicate and later became an author and teacher. God's design of senses is something to marvel at.

When we follow Jesus as our Savior, we have a special super sense. It's not like the catfish's taste buds, nostril sensors, or Weberian apparatus—it's much more powerful. God's Holy Spirit might nudge you to help someone in need or warn you of a dangerous situation or idea. Just as we can practice using a sense to make it stronger, we can become better at sensing God's Spirit. Romans 8:14 says God's children are led by God's Spirit. Like a catfish following its super sensors to find what it needs, God's Spirit will guide us into all truth and goodness.

Following God's Spirit is not always easy. Somctimes the world around us or our own minds can be noisy and we don't hear the Spirit's promptings. But we can practice becoming increasingly sensitive to God's Spirit at work in and around us, as Galatians 5:25 says: "Since we live by the Spirit, let us keep in step with the Spirit" (NIV).

Dear God, thank you for giving catfish super sensors. It's so neat to see all your designs. We are glad creation is not boring but full of new discoveries around every corner. Help us to become more sensitive to your Spirit and to follow wherever you lead. Amen.

50

Grasshopper

Leap of Faith

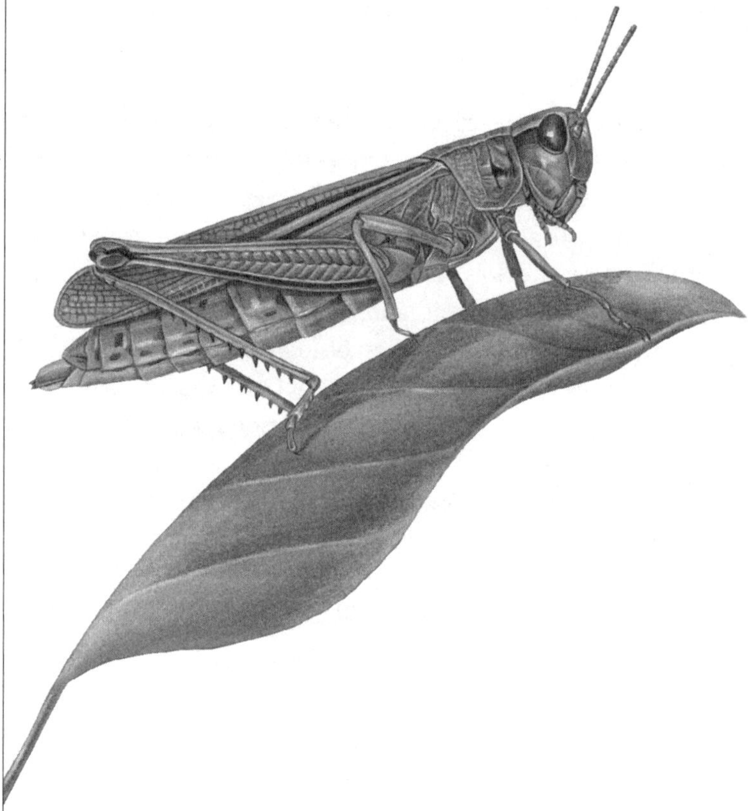

A Growing Grasshopper

My son once discovered a grasshopper in our yard that was in the middle of its molting process. The grasshopper had outgrown its exoskeleton, which acts like a backbone, giving the insect shape since it has no bones. As grasshoppers molt, they grow small wing buds, which resemble short pads along their back that look a little silly and certainly are unable to help them fly. Grasshoppers typically molt five to six times before emerging the final time as adults with fully developed wings that can fly.

My son held up a branch from our yard on which a grasshopper clung, or to be more accurate, the nearly empty shell of a grasshopper hung. The old shell still had some of its markings. We could see the black lines across the grasshopper's back and the braided design on its hind legs, but the shell itself was turning translucent, or see-through. From the shell hung the actual grasshopper, now much larger. Its head faced toward the ground as its long abdomen hung vertically. We could see the fresh wings lying flat along its back. This adult grasshopper had just emerged from its final molt and was getting ready to use its wings for the first time. But how does a grasshopper use its wings?

Grasshoppers Take Flight

Perhaps you have walked through a field and seen what you thought was a butterfly flitting by in the air, only to watch it land and discover it was not a butterfly at all but a grasshopper. While grasshoppers are famous jumpers, they are also excellent flyers. Like beetles, grasshoppers have a double set of wings. The first set, which we often see, is the forewings, and it is a more rigid, protective covering for the second set of wings, called the hindwings. The hindwings are the wings a grasshopper uses to fly, and they remain folded and protected beneath the outer forewings until they take flight. If you see a grasshopper flying, watch carefully to glimpse colors and patterns on its hindwings.

While grasshoppers typically fly low and short distances, some species, such as locusts, can fly high in the air and up to ninety miles a day as they migrate to find food.

Whether it's a short flight across a yard to escape a house cat's watchful eye or a long journey across hundreds of miles to find food, a grasshopper's flight is wonderfully designed and worth our attention. But how do they take to the skies in the first place?

Catapult Legs

Many birds launch into flight using upward lift or by trapping air beneath their wings and pushing that air downward. Bats often take flight by dropping themselves into the air from a high position, such as a tree. But how do grasshoppers take flight? The answer lies in their powerful legs, which act like catapults. A grasshopper's back legs are designed to fling its body into the sky, where its wings can take over.

Have you ever watched a grasshopper getting ready to jump? If you observe one carefully, you can glimpse God's magnificent engineering. First, the grasshopper pulls each of its back legs together. It does this using a special part of its leg called a ***femorotibial joint***, which is similar to our knees. This is kind of like bending your knee to bring the lower part of your leg tightly against the upper part, as when you sit on your knees. The grasshopper uses its special knee-like joint to lock its leg in a ready position. When a grasshopper does this, it stores up an incredible amount of energy in the muscle around the leg joint. As it jumps, that energy is released, and the grasshopper flings itself into the air. This is a lot like a slingshot's elastic cord pulled back to store energy to hurl a stone through the air, or the string of a drawn bow holding energy to shoot an arrow.

With this incredible engineering, a grasshopper can jump up to twenty times the length of its body. If an adult human jumped with the same power, it would be like clearing 120 feet in one leap or jumping the length of three school buses parked bumper to bumper.

Time to Explore

Explore a grassy area or field to find grasshoppers. Can you slowly and quietly approach to see one up close without it jumping away? Notice its large compound eyes and the braided design on its hind legs. Can you see one bending its femorotibial joint and locking its back legs into place, preparing to jump?

See how far you can jump. Stand in place and mark the floor with masking tape or a stick. From a standing position, jump as far as you can and mark where you land. Measure how far you jumped and marvel at how God designed grasshoppers to leap great lengths without a running start.

Leap of Faith

Do you think as a grasshopper catapults itself into the air, that it knows exactly where its leap will take it? It likely cannot picture the precise leaf or inch of ground it will land on.

We can at times feel like a grasshopper leaping into the air without knowing what's coming next. We might go through significant changes in life or face a challenge and not be able to picture what's ahead. However, even when a grasshopper leaps into the unknown, it can rely on its past experiences and the genius engineering of its legs.

We, too, can trust what we know to be true as we leap into unfamiliar territory. Abraham trusted as he followed God into an unknown land and future. Hebrews 11:8 says, "It was by faith Abraham obeyed God's call to go to another place God promised to give him. He left his own country, not knowing where he was to go." God faithfully led Abraham, and he guides us too.

It can be scary trying something new or facing a big change or challenge, but we can step forward boldly as we follow God's plan, knowing his ways are for our good and his glory. Psalm 37:23 assures us, "The LORD makes firm the steps of the one who delights in him" (NIV). As we delight in God and his plans, we can live by his design, just like a grasshopper leaping into the air while relying on the solid engineering of its legs.

The next time you feel uncertain about what lies ahead, remember 2 Corinthians 5:7: "We live by what we believe, not by what we can see."

Even when we cannot see every detail of the path ahead, we can trust God's design and plan.

Dear God, you smartly made grasshoppers able to jump and land. You have a smart design for our lives too. Help us to trust you when we feel unsure about the future and to follow where you lead, knowing you have given us all we need to follow your plan. Amen.

51

Deer Fawn

Never Alone

Speckled Fawns

Have you ever seen a deer baby, called a fawn, with white spots? The speckled appearance is a clear giveaway that the fawn is young. God dressed deer fawns in white speckles to help them blend in with their surroundings so predators, such as wolves, coyotes, and mountain lions, cannot find them. White speckles break up the solid brown of a fawn's body and look more like dappled light on grass or across bushes.

Fawns are born in late spring or early summer. They begin to lose their speckles around three to four months old, as they molt for the first time, shedding their hair so they can grow a new, thicker winter coat to keep them warm in the colder months.

On Their Own

Have you ever seen a fawn on its own or heard a story of someone finding a fawn? People get concerned if they find a fawn without its mother. Fawns look small and fragile, like they should not be left to fend for themselves. However, fawns are left on their own for an essential purpose: That's how their mothers keep them safe.

For the first few weeks of life, a doe (female deer) will often leave her fawn for hours at a time. She guides her fawn to a hidden space where it will not be noticed. At this young age, the fawn cannot move very fast. If the mother and baby travel together, they can easily be seen by a predator and cannot make a quick getaway. So, the mother hides her fawn and leaves to go find the nutrition she needs to keep her strong and able to feed her baby. The mother will visit the fawn throughout the day to nurse it with milk.

God has given ***instincts*** to animal mothers, such as deer, to know how to best care for their young. Instincts are natural behaviors that animals (and people) are born with the knowledge and ability to use. They don't have to be taught.

As humans, our instinct is to stay with a newborn baby and never leave it on its own. But God has given a mother deer a different instinct to protect her baby in the wild. A deer mother knows the best way to safeguard her fawn is to leave it in a safe hiding place.

If you find a fawn on its own in late spring or early summer, it is best to leave it alone. Its mother is likely nearby and will return soon to check on and care for her baby.

Growing Up

As a fawn grows bigger and stronger, it will begin following its mother on foraging trips. I recently watched a mother mule deer guide her two fawns down a forested hillside to a creek below for a drink of water. The fawns followed close behind their mother. If they became distracted by a good patch of grass and got a bit too far away, they would run to catch up with their mother. The mother paid close attention to the forest around them. She was on the lookout for any potential dangers and was ready at a moment's notice to bound away with her babies.

Fawns will stay with their mother for around one year. They only nurse from their mother for about two to three months. After that, they begin eating grass and other plants. They remain with their mother, learning how to stay safe, while finding all the food and water they need.

Time to Explore

Find a place where deer often visit and plan a morning to watch them. Mule deer in the American West prefer forests and mountainous hillsides. White-tailed deer are usually found by rivers and in fields. Deer are most active at dawn and dusk. Try to find a mother deer with her fawn. Does the fawn still have spots, or has it grown its first winter coat? How do the mother and fawn interact?

Never Alone

It seems strange and even wrong to us that a mother deer leaves her new fawn by itself for hours at a time. However, the fawn is never truly alone. The mother remains in the area and is always aware of her fawn's location, returning several times each day to nurse her baby.

Similarly, we can sometimes feel as though God has left us by ourselves. Have you ever wondered if God is hearing your prayers or if he is close by?

Just like a deer mother stays near her fawn, God is never far from us. Take comfort in these promises from God's Word:

- "Be strong and brave. Don't be afraid of them and don't be frightened, because the LORD your God will go with you. He will not leave you or forget you." (Deut. 31:6)
- "So don't worry, because I am with you." (Isa. 41:10)
- "And I will be with you always, even until the end of this age." (Matt. 28:20)
- "God is our refuge and strength, an ever-present help in trouble." (Ps. 46:1 NIV)

Reread the last verse. What do you think it means that God is "ever-present"? God is always near and ready to help, just like a deer who knows right where her fawn is and is ready to care for her little one.

Dear God, thank you for giving deer the instincts to care for their babies. Thank you for never being far from us but always close by and ready to help. Amen.

52

Bee

Seeing the Unseen

Created with Purpose

Have you ever seen a bee collecting nectar from a flower? A ***forager bee*** gathering food is only a small glimpse of the workload of a beehive.

Worker bees change jobs as they get older, beginning as cleaner bees, who keep the hive neat and tidy, then they move on to care for bee babies, called larvae. Around eighteen to twenty days of age, they are promoted to guard bees, who help to keep the hive safe. Around twenty days after hatching, worker bees begin their first ***orientation flights***, flying around the hive to become familiar with their surroundings. The bees map certain landmarks so they can find their way home when they venture farther. Once they learn the landscape, they become forager bees, responsible for finding the sweet nectar and pollen the hive needs.

If there is a need in the hive, a bee can change back to a previous role to give help where necessary. Bees are designed to perform each job well, just as God has called each of us to meaningful work and gives us everything we need to carry out that work, as 2 Corinthians 9:8 says, "And God is able to bless you abundantly, so that in all things at all times, having all that you need, you will abound in every good work" (NIV).

A Sophisticated Design

Have you ever heard the word ***sophisticated***? Sophisticated can mean something is designed very smartly and with many details. It is not simple. A sophisticated design works well, and we certainly see that in a beehive! Watching bees go about their daily work, we can glimpse God's handiwork and wisdom. How are bees designed in detail? Here are three fascinating examples:

- Honeybees have tiny ***pollen baskets*** for carrying pollen on the go! In science, these are called ***corbiculae***, which are structures on a bee's leg that are surrounded by little hairs. Pollen sticks to the corbiculae so the bee can bring it back to the hive.
- Forager bees perform a skilled ***waggle dance*** in a figure eight motion to communicate to their hivemates where a good source of nectar is located.

- Bees have five eyes, which act more like thousands of eyes. They have three simpler eyes called ***ocelli*** on the top of their head that help them sense light and dark. The two larger eyes we see are ***compound eyes*** designed with thousands of tiny lenses to give them a wide field of vision and to help them sense motion, which allows them to react quickly.

The above examples do not even come close to sharing all the wonders of bees. To do so would fill many books. Their complexity reminds me of the Bible, when John writes about the works Jesus did on earth. He shared this thought in John 21:25: "Jesus did many other things as well. If every one of them were written down, I suppose that even the whole world would not have room for the books that would be written" (NIV). The same could be said of the wonderful ways God designed creatures, including bees. We can explore creation and learn more each day. Still, on this side of eternity, we'll never fully grasp the magnitude of God's wonderful works.

Unique Color Vision

With their smartly designed eyes, bees see colors differently than humans do. While bees do not see the color red, they do see a color called ***bee purple***, which is a mix of yellow and ultraviolet light that we cannot see. Along with the bee, God designed other creatures with color vision that is different from our own. As an example, the mantis shrimp living in the ocean has up to sixteen color sensors, compared to a human's three color sensors, and it can see magnificent colors we cannot even imagine. What do you think the world looks like to a mantis shrimp or a bee?

Time to Explore

Watch a bee working hard. Give them space so they don't feel threatened and you don't risk getting stung. An area with many flowers is a great place to observe and appreciate bees. Can you see powdery pollen on the bees' legs? If you see a bright clump of it on the back of their legs, you've spotted their pollen basket! Do you see any bees climbing deep within a tube-shaped flower to get the sweet nectar inside? Thank God for designing bees so smartly that they can spread pollen, allowing more plants to grow.

Seeing the Unseen

It is hard to imagine what we have never seen. And yet, as we discovered, bees see a color we cannot. There are things in nature that human eyes do not perceive.

Over the years, many scientists who do not believe in God have argued that the only things that are real are things that can be seen and touched (material things). Yet the more people discover in nature and science, the more we see that this is not true. An example is something called ***dark matter*** and dark energy. Scientists are still uncertain what these two things actually are, but they know they are real and invisible. According to NASA, around 95 percent of the universe is made of these two invisible things.* What more might exist in the universe that we cannot see?

Colossians 1:16 says, "For in him all things were created: things in heaven and on earth, visible and invisible" (NIV). Imagine everything in creation that we cannot see!

First Corinthians 13:12 tells us, "Now we see things imperfectly, like puzzling reflections in a mirror, but then we will see everything with perfect clarity. All that I know now is partial and incomplete, but then I will know everything completely, just as God now knows me completely" (NLT).

We see only part of what God has made. Creatures like bees and the mantis shrimp can see things we cannot. As we follow Jesus, let's keep discovering everything we can as we explore God's wild and wonderful world. And let's look forward to the day when we will see so much more fully, marveling at things we cannot even imagine!

Dear God, thank you for thoughtfully designing bees and for making us wonderfully, with important work to do. Thank you for everything you have made, both the things we can see and the things we cannot. The world is full of your wonders beyond what we can imagine! Amen.

* Chelsea Gohd, "What Is Dark Matter?," NASA, updated August 29, 2025, https://science.nasa.gov/dark-matter/.

Explore by Topic

Glossary

American Robin

chick: A baby bird.

fledge: When a young bird leaves its nest.

fledgling: A young bird that has left its nest.

syrinx: A special voice box in some songbirds that has a double set of vocal cords and can produce two distinct sounds simultaneously.

thrush: A category of birds that includes the American robin, hermit thrush, and wood thrush.

Ant

colony: A group of ants that live and work together—with a queen and workers—to build the nest, find food, and protect their home.

communicate: Share information.

sensilla: Tiny hairlike sensors on an insect's antennae (or body) that help it smell, feel, or sense what's around it.

Bat

echolocation: A way animals (like bats) find things in the dark by making sounds and listening to the echoes to know what and where objects are.

mammal: A category of animals that have hair or fur, are warm-blooded, and have a backbone; most give birth to live young and nurse their babies with milk.

tragus: A small flap or bump at the front of the ear opening that helps collect sound—in bats, it helps them hear echoes for echolocation.

uropatagium: The thin skin between a bat's back legs and tail that helps it catch insects while flying. Also called the **interfemoral membrane**.

Bear Scat

carnivore lethargy: A bear's long winter rest in a safe den where it sleeps most of the time, uses little energy, and lives mostly off body fat until spring; different from true hibernation. Also called **denning**.

hyperphagia: A time of extreme hunger when an animal (like a bear) eats a huge amount of food to build up fat before winter.

satisfied: To be pleased and content, not wanting more.

Bee

bee purple: A color made from yellow and ultraviolet light that bees can see and humans cannot.

compound eye: A special kind of eye made of many tiny lenses that help insects (like bees) see in detail.

dark matter: Unseen stuff in space that scientists believe makes up most of the universe's matter.

forager bee: A worker bee that's responsible for finding flowers and bringing nectar and pollen back to the hive.

ocelli: Simple eyes many insects have on top of their head that help them sense light and dark.

orientation flights: The first flights a worker bee takes around its hive to learn its surroundings.

pollen baskets: Special structures on a bee's legs that pollen sticks to so a bee can carry loads of pollen back to the hive. Also called **corbiculae**.

sophisticated: Designed with knowledge and detail (complexity).

waggle dance: A figure eight flight pattern that forager bees use to communicate to hivemates where a good source of nectar is located.

Beetle

elytra: The hard outer front wings of a beetle that protect its body and inner wings.

exoskeleton: A hard outer shell on a creature without a backbone (like an insect) that protects it and gives it shape.

pupal state: A resting stage when an insect is inside a protective covering and changing into an adult.

Canada Goose

echelon: A formation where animals, people, or vehicles are arranged in a line or pattern—each one slightly behind and to the side of the one in front.

updraft: A rising flow of air created when something—like a bird's wings—pushes air downward.

Catfish

barbels: Long, whisker-like feelers around a catfish's mouth that help it sense and taste its surroundings.

olfactory rosettes: Folded, ribbonlike structures inside a catfish's nose that are covered in smell sensors to help it detect scents in the water.

Weberian apparatus: A set of tiny bones in some fish that connects the swim bladder to the inner ear so sound vibrations can be heard better.

Cattail

growth node: A small part of a plant's stem where new growth occurs, including branches, buds, and leaves.

Chipmunk

***Tamias*:** The genus name for chipmunks; it comes from Greek and means "steward," "treasurer," or "collector" because chipmunks store lots of food.

Crayfish

abdomen: The rear part of a body behind the head and middle part.

caridoid escape reaction: A super-fast tail snap that shoots a crayfish backward to escape danger. Also called a **tail-flip**.

neurons: Tiny message-carrying cells that send signals through an animal's body, to the brain and back.

swimmerets: Small, feathery structures under a crayfish's abdomen that help it swim and hold its eggs.

Crow

***Corvidae*:** A family of intelligent, problem-solving birds that includes crows, ravens, blue jays, and magpies.

influence: When actions or words impact how someone else thinks, feels, or acts.

Daddy Longlegs

***Arachnida*:** The class of creatures that includes spiders, scorpions, and daddy longlegs.

***Araneae*:** Order of all spiders.

cephalothorax: The front part of some creatures' bodies where the head and chest are joined together as one piece.

discernment: Being able to tell what is right and true from what is wrong or false.

***Opiliones*:** Order of all daddy longlegs, also often called harvestmen.

stomotheca (pronounced stow-moe-THEE-ca): The unique mouthpart on daddy longlegs designed for crushing and chewing solid food.

Daisy

composite flower: A single flower head made of many tiny flowers arranged together on one stem (like a daisy or sunflower).

cross-pollination: When pollen is carried from one flower to another (often by insects), helping plants make seeds.

disk flowers: The tiny flowers in the center disk of a composite flower.

Fibonacci spiral: A special spiral pattern found in nature following a mathematical sequence.

hermeneutics: The study and interpretation of the Bible.

ray flowers: The petallike flowers around the outside edge of a composite flower. Also called **banner flowers**.

self-pollination: When a flower uses its own pollen to make seeds.

Deer Fawn

instincts: Natural behaviors that animals (and people) are born knowing how to do—they don't have to be taught.

Dragonfly

direct flight muscle: A muscle that is attached to one wing and moves just that wing.

forewings: The front pair of wings on an insect with four wings.

hindwings: The back pair of wings on an insect with four wings.

leading-edge vortex: A small, spinning swirl of air (like a tiny tornado) made at the front edge of a wing that gives an insect extra lift to stay in the air.

Earthworm

aerating: Loosening soil so air can get into it, which helps plants grow.

castings: Worm poop that is full of nutrients and acts like natural fertilizer for plants.

hydrostat muscles: Special muscles working with water in animals without bones (like worms) that help the body stretch, squeeze, and move, acting like a soft skeleton.

segments: Ringlike body sections on a worm that let it stretch and move through soil.

setae (pronounced SEE-tee): Tiny hairlike bristles on a worm's body that help it grip and move.

Fern

fiddlehead: A young fern frond that is still curled up in a spiral.

fractal: A pattern that repeats its shape over and over, even when you zoom in—big, medium, and tiny.

frond: The whole leafy part of a fern on one stem.

pinnae: The leaflet parts that grow along the sides of a fern frond.

pinnules: The tiny leaf parts that make up each pinna.

sporangia: Small round or oval packets on the underside of a fern frond that hold and release spores to make new ferns.

Firefly

bioluminescence (pronounced bye-o-loom-in-ESS-enz): Meaning "living light"; a chemical reaction in some creatures that creates light.

luciferase: An enzyme that breaks down the luciferin molecule to create living light.

luciferin: A molecule used in bioluminescence.

thorax: The middle part of an insect's body where the legs and wings attach.

Fireweed

rhizomes: A special kind of plant stem that grows sideways underground, not above the soil.

wind dispersal: When seeds are carried to a new area by wind.

Fog

fog drip: Water droplets that form from fog on leaves and then drip to the ground, bringing moisture to plant roots.

water cycle: The way water moves around Earth, evaporating into the air, forming clouds, falling as rain or snow, and going back to rivers, lakes, and oceans to start the cycle again.

Fool's Gold (Pyrite)

luster: The way a mineral's surface reflects light—how shiny or dull it looks.

malleable: Able to be bent, hammered, or pressed into a new shape without breaking.

pyritized fossil: A fossil where the original hard parts (like shell or bone) have been replaced by pyrite, making it look golden.

sediment: Small pieces of rock, sand, soil, or other natural material that are carried by water, wind, or ice and then settle in a new place.

Fox

biological control: A living thing that helps control (or reduce) another living thing that could cause problems.

***Canidae*:** The dog family that includes wolves, jackals, foxes, coyotes, and domestic (pet or working) dogs.

crepuscular: Mostly active at dawn and dusk.

kits: Baby foxes.

reputation: What people tend to think about a person, normally because of the way they act.

Frog

brumation: A cold-weather rest where cold-blooded creatures (like reptiles and amphibians) move very little to save energy.

glucose: A sugar compound in living things.

metabolism: How a body breaks down food into nutrients for energy to live, move, and grow.

suspended animation: An extreme state of rest where an animal's body almost completely shuts down so it can survive harsh conditions and return to normal activity later.

Garter Snake

Jacobson's organ: A special scent organ inside a snake's mouth that reads scent particles from its tongue and sends information to the brain about what it is smelling.

membrane: A thin, soft, stretchy covering that protects a baby animal.

ovoviviparous (pronounced oh-voh-vih-VIP-er-us): When babies grow inside eggs that stay inside the mother's body and the babies are born live.

snakelets: Baby snakes.

***Thamnophis*:** A genus that includes around thirty-five species of garter snakes.

Grasshopper

femorotibial joint: A grasshopper's knee-like joint where the upper leg meets the lower leg, used to bend and lock the leg for storing energy before jumping.

Great Blue Heron

colony birds: Birds that nest and raise their young together in groups.

crest: A group of feathers on top of a bird's head that can stand up or lie flat, often used to show mood or to help the bird look bigger.

nuptial plumes: Long, fancy feathers that grow on a bird during breeding season to attract a mate or impress other birds.

rookery: An area where different species of birds nest together.

Loon

voiceprint: A one-of-a-kind sound pattern in an animal's call (like a male loon's yodel) that makes it distinguishable from all others.

Monarch Chrysalis

carotenoid: A color pigment found throughout nature causing red, orange, and yellow coloring in plants and creatures.

chrysalis: A hard, protective case a caterpillar makes from its own body to rest in while it transforms into a butterfly.

eclosing: When a butterfly emerges from its chrysalis.

molt: To shed an old outer covering, such as fur or an exoskeleton.

Mouse

allocentric navigation: Finding your way by using landmarks around you to know where you are and which direction to go.

egocentric navigation: Finding your way by remembering your own turns and movements (like "right," "left," "straight").

spatial memory: The ability to remember where things are and how to get to them.

Oak Tree

cell membrane: A thin, flexible covering around an animal or human cell that holds everything inside.

cell wall: A strong, rigid outer layer around a plant cell that helps the plant stand upright.

cells: Tiny building blocks of living things that work like little factories to keep them alive and growing.

cellulose: Strong plant fibers in the cell wall that help plants stand upright.

lignin: A natural glue-like substance in plants that makes wood and stems hard and strong.

secondary cell wall: An extra-strong layer inside a plant cell that makes the plant tougher.

Owl

anastomoses: A backup route of blood vessels that can reroute blood between main arteries.

arteries: Tubes that carry oxygen-rich blood from the heart to the rest of the body.

neck vertebrae: Neck bones.

Petrichor

geosmin: Meaning "earth-smell"; a chemical mixture made when specific bacteria in the soil break down dead things; rain releases this chemical mixture into the air and makes the ground smell fresh.

Pill Bug

***Armadillidiidae*:** The scientific name for pill bugs.

common name: The everyday nicknames people use, which can be different in various places.

decomposer: A creature that eats dead plants or animals and turns them into nutrients for the soil.

negative phototaxis: An instinct in some creatures to move away from light and seek out dark places.

scientific name: The official name scientists use worldwide so everyone knows exactly which creature or plant they're talking about.

terrestrial crustacean: A crustacean that lives on land instead of in water.

Pitcher Plant

bog: A very wet, spongy natural area made of sphagnum moss and decaying plants, with acidic soil that has few nutrients, where few types of plants can grow.

carnivorous plant: A plant that traps and eats insects to get extra nutrients.

enzyme: Special proteins that help speed up certain chemical reactions in living organisms, such as breaking down food into smaller parts the body can use.

mutualistic relationship: When two living things help each other and both benefit.

sphagnum moss: A soft, spongelike plant that grows in very wet places (like bogs) and holds lots of water.

Rabbit

forms: A rabbit's favorite soft, grassy resting spots where it sits or hides.

home territory: The area where an animal usually lives, eats, and knows all the safe spots.

***Lagomorpha*:** The animal order that includes rabbits, hares, and pikas.

olfactory sensors: Tiny smell detectors inside the nose that pick up scents and send them to the brain.

Raccoon

nocturnal: Creatures that are active mostly during the night.

***Procyon lotor*:** Scientific name for the common raccoon, meaning "washer."

tapetum lucidum (pronounced tuh-PEE-tum LOO-sih-dum): A reflective layer in the eyes of most mammals that creates a glowing or shining effect.

Salamander

cutaneous respiration: A way some animals breathe by taking in oxygen through their skin instead of their lungs.

***ex nihilo* (pronounced ex NEE-huh-low):** A Latin phrase meaning "out of nothing" or "from nothing."

larvae: The young stage of some animals, like insects and amphibians, that go through metamorphosis.

metamorphosis: The process by which an insect or amphibian changes from its immature (baby) form to its adult form through a series of stages.

spontaneous generation: Past idea in science that living things appeared from nonliving things.

vernal pond: A temporary pond that contains water for only part of the year and is a unique ecosystem for creatures, including amphibians.

Sand

erosion: When natural processes like rain, wind, or crashing waves wear away rock and soil.

white quartz: A common mineral, often found in rocks, made of silicon and oxygen that looks white, milky, or cloudy.

Skunk

gland: A special part of an animal's body that makes and releases important substances like liquids or chemicals.

Musteloidea: A large group of mammals that includes skunks, weasels, mink, and otters; many members of this group have scent glands.

Snapping Turtle

ambush predator: An animal that hides or stays very still and then attacks quickly when prey comes close.

vermiform lure: A worm-shaped part on the alligator snapping turtle's tongue that it wiggles to attract prey.

Sunfish

***Centrarchiformes*:** An order of fish often called sunfish and including smallmouth and largemouth bass along with bluegill.

chromatophores: Cells in a fish's skin that hold pigments (like red, yellow, brown) and give the fish its color.

fry: Baby fish.

iridophores: Shiny cells with tiny crystals that reflect light and make the fish look sparkly or metallic.

Sunflower

auxin: A special plant hormone that makes cells on the shady side of a plant grow longer so the plant can bend toward the sun.

chlorophyll: The green pigment in plants that helps them soak up sunlight to make food.

heliotropism: A plant's directional growth in response to sunlight.

hormones: Tiny chemical messengers that tell a plant what to do, like when to grow, make flowers, or make more chlorophyll.

photosynthesis: The process plants use to turn sunlight, water, and air into food so they can grow.

Termite

castes: Different groups (such as in termite or ant colonies) with special jobs—like a teamwork system.

colony: A group of termites living and working together.

protozoa: Tiny, single-celled living organisms.

reproductives: The male and female termites that mate in flight and are the future kings and queens of the colony.

Thistle

exotic plant: A plant growing outside its natural ecosystem.

invasive plants: A native or exotic plant that dominates an area and crowds out other plants.

native plant: A plant that is growing in its natural habitat.

thistle bird: A nickname for goldfinches, inspired by their reliance on thistles for food and nesting material.

thistledown: A soft, silklike material attached to seedheads that helps seeds spread by wind.

Tree Bark

heartwood: The hard, inner wood at the center of a tree trunk that supports the tree.

inner bark: A layer beneath the outer bark that delivers food throughout the tree and grows the inner wood and outer bark.

outer bark: The protective layer on the outside of a tree that defends the tree against invaders.

Vulture

carrion: Decaying flesh of dead animals.

scavenger: Birds or other creatures that eat carrion (animals that are already dead) instead of hunting live prey.

Wild Grass

anthers: The parts of a flower that hold pollen.

perennial: A plant that grows back every spring.

***Poaceae*:** The plant family of grasses—plants with hollow stems, long narrow leaves, and roots that spread to hold soil together.

seedhead: The brush or featherlike top part of a grass plant where seeds grow.

spikelet: A tiny, wrapped cluster of flowers on a grass plant.

Wind

ballooning: When a spider lets out silk and uses the wind to lift and carry it through the air, like a tiny parachute.

electric field: An invisible force around our planet that comes from electric charges.

thermal: A rising column of warm air.

Want to learn even more? Explore each *Made to Marvel* topic further with related *Nat Theo* podcast lessons at TheNaturalTheologyProject.com /Marvel.

Acknowledgments

Creator God, you gave me an endless supply of inspiration and materials when you said "Let there be . . ." back at creation. Discovering and sharing your creation is a joy.

Grayson, thank you for constantly inspiring me to marvel at God's creation. Thank you for listening to all my science facts and for sharing new ones with me. I'm so grateful for all the ways you made this project possible.

Zeke, Ellis, Will, and Aurora, thank you for introducing me to so much of what is in this book. Every time you say, "Mom, come see this!" you invite me into your world of wonder. Never stop marveling at God's creation. And please keep inviting me to come along on the adventure.

Mom, thank you for joyfully offering your time so I could focus on and complete this manuscript. I wish Dad had had the chance to read it, but I know it would bring him great joy. The two of you have always inspired me to marvel at God's creation. Thank you.

Jill Smith, your curiosity for God's creation is contagious. The joy in your voice and eyes as you share about his wonders is powerful. Thank you for your careful review of the science in these pages. I love learning from you.

Bob Hostetler of the Steve Laube Agency and Andrea Doering and the Revell Team, thank you for seeing the need and vision for this work.

About the Author

ERYN LYNUM is a certified Master Naturalist, educator, and national speaker. Eryn hosts the popular podcast for families, *Nat Theo: Nature Lessons Rooted in the Bible*. She is the author of five books including *Made to Marvel*, *Where Wonder Leads*, *The Nature of Rest*, *Rooted in Wonder*, and *936 Pennies*. She lives in Northern Colorado with her husband, Grayson, and their four children, whom they homeschool. Every opportunity she gets, she is out exploring God's creation and sharing the wonders of what he's made.

Connect with Eryn:

TheNaturalTheologyProject.com

Facebook @AuthorErynLynum

Instagram @ErynLynumAuthor